PREFATORY NOTE.

THE first, second, fifth, and sixth of the Essays included in the present volume are reprinted from
a volume published by the Author in 1856 under
the title *Essays Biographical and Critical: chiefly on
English Poets.* The Essays on Shelley and Keats
are now added. Two similar volumes of revised
Essays will follow; the next of which will be
Chatterton: A Story of the Year 1770.

EDINBURGH :
    April 1874.

WORDSWORTH, SHELLEY, KEATS,

AND

OTHER ESSAYS.

WORDSWORTH, SHELLEY, KEATS,

AND

OTHER ESSAYS.

BY

DAVID MASSON

NEW EDITION.

Essay Index Reprint Series

First Published 1875
Reprinted 1973

Library of Congress Cataloging in Publication Data

Masson, David, 1822-1907.
   Wordsworth, Shelley, Keats, and other essays.

   (Essay index reprint series)
   Reprint of the 1875 ed.
 ' 1.   English literature--Addresses, essays, lectures.
I.   Title.
PR99.M327   1973   820'.9   72-13205
ISBN 0-8369-8168-5

CONTENTS.

I.

WORDSWORTH.

B

ESSAYS.

I.

WORDSWORTH.[1]

ANOTHER great spirit has recently gone from the midst of us. It is now three months since the nation heard, with a deep though quiet sadness, that an aged man of venerable mien, who for fifty years had borne worthily the name of English poet, had at length disappeared from those scenes of lake and mountain where, in stately care of his own worth, he had fixed his recluse abode, and passed forward, one star the more, into the still unfeatured future, whither all that lives is rolling, and whither, as he well knew and believed, the Shakespeares and Miltons, whom men count dead, had but as yesterday transferred their kindred radiance. When the news spread, it seemed as if our island were

---

[1] *North British Review*, August 1850.—" The Poetical Works of William Wordsworth, D.C.L., Poet Laureate, &c." London, 1849.

suddenly a man the poorer, as if some pillar or other
notable object, long conspicuous on its broad surface,
had suddenly fallen down.   It is right, then, that we
should detain our thoughts for a little in the vicinity
of this event ; that, the worldly course of such a man
having now been ended, we should stand for a little
around his grave, and think solemnly of what he was.
Neither few nor unimportant, we may be sure, are the
reflections that should suggest themselves over the
grave of William Wordsworth.

Of the various mysteries that the human mind can
contemplate none is more baffling, and at the same time
more charming to the understanding, than the nature of
that law which determines the differences of power and
mental manifestation between age and age.   That all
history is an evolution, that each generation inherits
all that had been accumulated by its predecessor, and
bequeathes in turn all that itself contains to its
successor, is an idea to which, in one form or another,
science binds us down.   But, native as this idea now is
in all cultivated minds, with how many facts, and with
what a large proportion of our daily speech, does it not
still stand in apparent contradiction !   Looking back
upon the past career of our race, does not the eye single
out, as by instinct, certain epochs that are epochs of
virtue and glory, and others that are epochs of frivolity

and shame? Do we not speak of the age of Pericles
in Greece, of the Augustan age in Rome, of the outburst of chivalry in modern Europe, of the noble era
of Elizabeth in England, and of the sad decrepitude
that followed it? And is there not a certain justice
of perception in this mode of speaking? Does it not
seem as if all ages were not equally favoured from on
high, gifts both moral and intellectual being vouch-
safed to one that are all but withheld from another?
As with individual men, so with nations and with
humanity at large, may not the hour of highest spiritual elevation and sternest moral resolve be nearest
the hour of most absolute obliviousness and most profound degradation? Has not humanity also its moods
—now brutal and full-acorned, large in physical device,
and pregnant with the wit of unconcern; again,
touched to higher things, tearful for very goodness,
turning an upward eye to the stars, and shivering to
its smallest nerve with the power and the sense of
beauty? In rude and superficial expression of which
fact, have not our literary men coined the commonplace that a critical and sceptical age always follows
an age of heroism and creative genius?

These, we say, are queries which, though they may
not be answered to their depths, it is still useful to put
and ponder. One remark only will we venture in connexion with them. According to one theory, it is a

sufficient explanation of these moral and intellectual changes in the spirit of nations to suppose that they take place. by a law of mere contagion or propagation from individual to individual. One man of powerful and original nature, or of unusually accurate perceptions, makes his appearance in some central, or, it may be, sequestered spot; he gains admirers or makes converts; disciples gather round him, or try to form an opinion of him from a distance; they, again, in their turn, affect others; till, at last, as the gloom of the largest church is slowly changed into brilliance by the successive lighting of all its lamps, so a whole country may, district by district, succumb to the peculiarity of a new influence! Now, this is perfectly true; and it would be indeed difficult to estimate the amazing efficacy of such a law of incessant diffusion from point to point over a surface. But this mode of representing the fact under notice does not convey the whole truth. Concerning even the silent pestilences, we have been recently taught that they do not wholly depend on transmission from individual to individual, but are rather distinct derangements in the body of the earth itself, tremors among its electricities and imponderables, alterations of the sum-total of those material conditions wherewith human life has been associated. In like manner, as it appears to us, must those streaming processes of sympathy and contagion whereby a moral or

intellectual change is diffused over a community be
regarded as but the superficial indications of a deep
contemporaneous agitation pervading the whole frame
of Nature. From the mineral core of this vast world,
outwards to the last thoughts, impulses, and conclusions
of us its human inhabitants, there runs, as science
teaches, a mystic law of intercourse and affinity,
pledging its parts to act in concert. The moral and
intellectual revolutions of our world, its wars, its new
philosophies, its outbursts of creative genius, its
profligate sinkings, and its noble recoveries, all must
rest, under the decree of supreme wisdom, on a con-
current basis of physical undulations and vicissitudes.
When, therefore, a man starts up in any locality,
charged with a new spirit or a new desire, there, be
sure, the ground around him is similarly affected.
New intellectual dispositions are like atmospheres;
they overhang whole countries at once. It is not
necessarily by communication or plagiarism that the
thought excogitated to-day in London breaks out to-
morrow in Edinburgh, or that persons in Göttingen and
Oxford are found speculating at the same time in the
same direction. In our own island, for example, it is
a fact capable of experimental verification, that whatever is being thought at any one time in any one spot,
is, with a very small amount of difference, being
independently thought at the same time in fifty other

places at all distances from each other. And yet it is equally true that in every moral or spiritual revolution there is always a leader, a forerunner, a man of originality, in whose individual bosom the movement seems to have been rehearsed and epitomized, and that in the beginning of every such revolution the power of contagion from man to man, and the machinery of the clique, school, or phalanx, must come into play.

These remarks are not too remote or abstract for the present occasion. The nineteenth century is a sufficiently large portion of historic time, England is a sufficiently large portion of the historic earth, and the poetical literature of England, or of any other nation, is a sufficiently important element in that nation's existence, to justify our viewing that remarkable phenomenon, *the Revival of English Poetry in the Nineteenth Century,* in the light of the most extreme general conceptions that can be brought to bear upon it. Against the preceding observations, therefore, as against what seems an appropriate background, let us try to bring out the main features of the phenomenon itself, so far, at least, as these can be exhibited with reference to the life and writings of its most " representative man." And first of Wordsworth regarded historically.

From Dryden till about fifty years ago (*i.e.* till about

1800), say our authorities in literary history, was an
era of poetical sterility in England. When Coleridge
gave lectures in London on the English poets, he
divided them into three lists or sections—the first,
including all the poets from Chaucer to Dryden; the
second, all those from Dryden inclusively to the close
of the eighteenth century; and the third, all those of
his own generation. The view presented by him of
the characters of these three periods, relatively to each
other, was essentially that conveyed in the strange
theory of alternate ebb and flow, alternate immission
and withdrawal of power, as regulating the progress
of the universe. In other words, the first period was
a period of strength, youth, and outburst; the second
was a period of cleverness, conceit, and poverty; and
the third was a period of revival. For, the poetic
spirit being one constant thing, a certain specific and
invariable quality or state of the human soul, not
capable of change from century to century, but the
same of old, now, and for ever, it follows that the
history of poetry can present no other appearance than
that of alternate presence and absence, alternate excess
and deficiency, alternate extinction and renovation.
That is to say—accepting the poetry of Chaucer and
Milton as true poetry, we cannot go on to defend
the poetry of Pope and Johnson as true poetry of
a different kind, and then, coming down to our own

age, assert that its poetry is true poetry of a different
kind still. Except in a very obvious sense, rendered
necessary by convenience, it cannot be said that there
are *kinds* of poetry. The materials on which the
poetic sense works are constantly varying; infinite,
also, are the combinations of human faculty and will
with which this sense may be structurally associated;
but the sense itself, whensoever and in whomsoever
it may be found, is still the same old thing that
trembled in the heart of Homer. An age may have
it or want it; may have more of it or less of it;
may have it in conjunction with this or with that
aggregate of other characteristics; but cannot abandon
one form of it and take up another.

In these remarks we have embodied a very necessary caution. If much good has been done by that
exaltation of meaning which the words Poet and Poetry
have received from the hands of Coleridge and others,
as well as by their kindred services in distinguishing
so constantly and so emphatically between the terms
reason and understanding, genius and talent, creation
and criticism, we are not quite sure but that, at the
same time, this infusion of new conceptions into our
language has been productive of some mischief. Agreeing, upon the whole, with the sentence of condemnation
which has been of late passed upon part of the poor
eighteenth century; believing that it was a critical.

negative, and unpoetic age; nay, even believing (however the belief is to be reconciled with the doctrine of
continuous historic evolution) that it was one of those
seasons of comparative diminution of the general vital
energy of our species which we have already spoken
of:—we still think that too sweeping a use has been
made of this notion and its accessories by a certain
class of writers. Let us illustrate our meaning by an
example. Keats, the poet, and James Mill, the historian of India, were contemporaries. The one, according to the language introduced by Coleridge, was
a man of genius; the other was a man of talent. In
the soul of Keats, if ever in a human soul at all, there
was a portion of the real poetic essence—the real
faculty divine; Mr. Mill, on the other hand, had
probably as little of the poet in his composition as any
celebrated man of his time, but he was a man of hard
metal, of real intellectual strength, and of unyielding
rectitude. In certain exercises of the mind he could
probably have crushed Keats, who was no weakling, as
easily as a giant could crush a babe. But, suppose the
two men to have sat together on Hampstead Heath in
a starry night, which of them would then have been
the stronger—which would have known the more
ecstatic pulses? Or, to make the case still more
decisive, suppose the two men to have been Keats and
Aristotle—Keats a consumptive poetic boy, and Aristotle

the intellect of half a world. Does not such a contrast bring out the real injustice that has been done to many truly great and good men by the habit which, since the time of Coleridge, has become general, of placing all the men that belong to the so-called category of genius in one united mass above all that rank only in the category of talent? For, though we may grant the reality of some such distinction as is implied between the two substantives, is it not clear that the general mass of mind possessed by a man reputed to belong to the inferior category, and consequently his general power to influence the soul of the world, may exceed a thousand times that possessed by a man of the other? In other words, may not a man rank so high in the one kind that, even though the kind itself be inferior, it may be said with truth that he is a hundred times greater a man than some specified lower man in the other? Practically, the tenor of these remarks is that we are in the present day committing an injustice by following the tendency of our young Coleridgians to restrict the meaning of the quantitative word "greatness" within the limits of the merely qualitative word "genius." And, speculatively, their tenor may be expressed in the proposition that this quality or mode of mind called genius, the poetic sense, creative power, and so on, may exist in association with all possible varieties of intellectual

or cerebral vigour, from the mediocrity of a Kirke
White or an Anacreon, up to the stupendousness of a
Shakespeare. It is thus that, while agreeing in the
main with the opinion that from Dryden to the close
of the next hundred years was a poetic interregnum,
we would still make our peace with those who would
fight the battle of the much-abused eighteenth century,
and would steer clear of the controversy whether Pope
was a poet. As deficiency in poetic power does not
imply corresponding deficiency in what may be called
ordinary cerebral vigour, so the eighteenth century,
though admitted to have been unpoetic, may have been
a very respectable century notwithstanding ; and, even
were we to exclude Pope from the class of poets (which
most certainly we would not do), we might still hold
him to have been a phenomenon in literature not, on
that account, a whit the less remarkable. A deeper
analysis would carry us farther into the question as
to the connexion between poetic power and general
intellect in individuals and in ages ; but here we
must stop.

Having thus explained in what sense we understand
that general assertion regarding the low state of English
poetry in the eighteenth century (part of the seven-
teenth included) with which the name of Wordsworth
is irrevocably associated, let us attend a little to the
facts of the case. In what did the sterility of English

poetry in that age consist, and what words would best
describe it? Here Wordsworth himself comes to our
aid. The following is from an Appendix to the Preface to the second edition of his *Lyrical Ballads,* published in 1800 : the subject under discussion is Poetic
Diction: —

"The earliest poets of all nations generally wrote
from passion excited by real events; they wrote naturally and as men : feeling powerfully as they did, their
language was daring and figurative. In succeeding
times, poets, and men ambitious of the fame of poets,
perceiving the influence of such language, and desirous
of producing the same effect without being animated
with the same passion, set themselves to a mechanical
adoption of these figures of speech, and made use of
them sometimes with propriety, but much more frequently applied them to feelings and thoughts with
which they had no natural connexion whatsoever. A
language was thus insensibly produced, differing mate-
rially from the real language of men in *any situation.*
The reader or hearer of this distorted language found
himself in a perturbed and unusual state of mind :
when affected by the genuine language of passion he
had been in a perturbed and unusual state of mind also:
in both cases he was willing that his common judgment
and understanding should be laid asleep, and he had no
instinctive and infallible perception of the true to make
him reject the false; the one served as a passport for
the other. The emotion was in both cases delightful;
and no wonder if he confounded the one with the

other, and believed them both to be produced by the
same or similar causes. Besides, the poet spake to him
in the character of a man to be looked up to, a man of
genius and authority. Thus, and from a variety of
other causes, this distorted language was received with
admiration; and poets, it is probable, who had before
contented themselves for the most part with misapplying
only expressions which at first had been dictated by
real passion, carried the abuse still further, and introduced phrases composed apparently in the spirit of the
original figurative language of passion, yet altogether
of their own invention, and characterised by various
degrees of wanton deviation from good sense and
nature. . . . Perhaps in no way, by positive example,
could be more easily given a notion of what I mean by
the phrase *poetic diction* than by referring to a comparison between the metrical paraphrases which we have of
passages in the Old and New Testament and those
passages as they exist in our common Translation. . . .
By way of immediate example, take the following of
Dr. Johnson :—

‘ Turn on the prudent Ant thy heedless eyes,
  Observe her labours, Sluggard, and be wise ;
  No stern command, no monitory voice,
  Prescribes her duties, or directs her choice ;
  Yet, timely provident, she hastes away
  To snatch the blessings of a plenteous day ;
  When fruitful Summer loads the teeming plain,
  She crops the harvest, and she stores the grain.
  How long shall sloth usurp thy useless hours,
  Unnerve thy vigour, and enchain thy powers ?

> While artful shades thy downy couch enclose,
> And soft solicitation courts repose,
> Amidst the drowsy charms of dull delight,
> Year chases year with unremitted flight,
> Till Want now following, fraudulent and slow,
> Shall spring to seize thee, like an ambush'd foe.'

From this hubbub of words pass to the original. 'Go to the Ant, thou Sluggard, consider her ways and be wise: which, having no guide, overseer, or ruler, provideth her meat in the summer, and gathereth her food in the harvest. How long wilt thou sleep, O Sluggard? when wilt thou arise out of thy sleep? Yet a little sleep, yet a little slumber, a little folding of the hands to sleep! So shall thy poverty come as one that travelleth, and thy want as an armed man.'"

To sum up the views thus presented by Wordsworth of the state of English poetry after Milton, it may be said that at that time the nation, having lost much of the genuine poetical power it had formerly possessed, but still preserving a form of composition to which it had been so long and so powerfully accustomed, began to regard the essence of poetry as lying in metre, accompanied by a certain peculiar and artificial phraseology called poetic diction, thus begetting that exaggerated antithesis between poetry and prose with which our language is still infected. Instead of regarding the poetic faculty as consisting in a mode or attitude of the mind, distinguishable, on the one hand, from the scientific mode or attitude, whose function is investigation or exposition, and, on the other hand, from the oratorical mode or attitude, whose function is to excite or stimulate in a particular direction, they made poetry to consist in a mode of language, and they estimated the value of a poet according to the degree of mastery he had attained in the use of this mode of language, and the degree of general mental power and resource he could manifest through it. Hence, in the first place, a gradual increase of departure in metrical composition from the idioms and combinations of words deemed appropriate to prose; and, in the second place, a gradual reduction of the range of metre itself to certain fixed varieties and methods of versification, which the older poets, who did not so much assort their thoughts to rhymes as let the thoughts flow out in their own rhythm, would have disdained as much as a natural cascade would disdain the assistance of pipes. But, while an exaggerated antithesis was thus established between prose and poetry, it by no means followed that a very wide separation was drawn between the devotees of the one and those of the other. Poetry was indeed a different form of diction from prose; but then, as it was not difficult for a clever man to acquire two forms of diction, one might very well be both a poet and a prose-writer! To pass from prose to poetry was but to pass from one's town to one's country house. Hence it was that so many of the literary men of last century had a reputation both in prose and in verse. General mental vigour carried an author triumphantly through either form of composition. Wit, sarcasm, strength, manliness, whatever qualities of intellect or disposition could earn respect for a writer in prose, were all capable —with a little training, or a slight native impulse towards the picturesque, to aid him—of being transfused into metre. The best poetry of the age was, accordingly, rather wit or reflection expressed in metre than real poetry in the strict sense of the word. And here lies the defence of the poets of that time, as well as their condemnation. Of many of them it may be denied that they were poets ; but of almost all of them it may be asserted that they were men of general mental vigour. In our disquisitions concerning them, therefore, let not this be forgotten. If Johnson was no poet, he was a very ponderous and noble old sage nevertheless ; and even the purists that would clip the laurels of Dryden and Pope must admit that now-a-days we have no such manly *literati* as the former about Leicester Square, and that the other was a diamond of the first water.

But the change came at length. By the mysterious operation of those laws which determine the risings and the sinkings of the mental state of humanity as a whole, there seemed to be effected, towards the close

of the eighteenth century, a sudden increase of the
vital energy of the species. Humanity assumed a
higher mood; a deep agitation, as if from a fresh
electric discharge out of celestial space into the solid
body of our planet, shook the soul of the world, and
left it troubled and excited. The two most conspicuous
and extensive manifestations of this heightened state
of the world's consciousness were—in the region of
speculation, the promulgation of the Transcendental
Philosophy in Germany, and, in the region of action,
the French Revolution. But, as if the same spirit
which burst forth in these two great eruptions also
sought vent through smaller and apparently uncon-
nected orifices all over Europe, there were not wanting
other significant indications of the change that was
taking place. In Germany, seemingly apart from
the Transcendental Philosophy, though in reality de-
riving strength from it through a subterranean conduit,
a new Literature came forth, under the care first of
Lessing, and then of Goethe. And in our own country,
sprinkled over as it had been in spots by the sound
and fertile philosophy of Reid, there was a feebler
exhibition of the same phenomenon. Even in the age
of reputed degeneracy there had been men of the true
poetic spark. Dryden and Pope may not have kept
it pure, but they assuredly had it; Gray, notwithstanding the dreadful disintegration to which his Elegy

c 2

has been submitted by modern critics, did certainly
possess the ear and sensibility of a poet; Collins and
Goldsmith were men of musical hearts; and Thomson,
Wordsworth himself being judge, was a genuine child
of rural nature. Nor here, whatever other names are left
unmentioned, let *him* be forgotten, the boy of Bristol,
the drunken choir-singer's posthumous son, who was
found dead in his garret in Brooke Street, Holborn,
on the 25th of August, 1770. But the real poetic
outburst came after these men had been removed from
the scene, and was plainly a consequence of that
general commotion of the earth to which we have
referred. Its earliest unmistakeable signs may be said
to have been given in the works of Cowper and Burns.
In the bard of Olney, invalid as he was, the new force
found an English mind that it could compel to speak
for it; and, when the swarthy Scottish ploughman
filled the Lowlands with his songs, it was clear that
the process of reformation had been completed, as
regarded this island, to its last spontaneous results,
and that every acre of the British earth had become
instinct and pregnant with the novel fire.

Accordingly, this was the period of the birth and
training of new English poets. Crabbe, Scott, Wordsworth, Coleridge, and Southey, were children of this
period; and in all of them—their peculiar differences
allowed for to the utmost—the new spirit was visible.

It was assigned to Wordsworth, however, more than to any other man, to be conscious of the fact that such a new spirit had been breathed into the world at all, and to conclude the process of its diffusion through society by bringing into play the powers of theoretical exposition through the press and personal influence over distinguished contemporaries.

Born among the Cumberland hills, in the year 1770— that is, in the year of Chatterton's death—Wordsworth was but eleven years younger than Burns. It is pleasant to think that these two men, though they never met, were near neighbours. From within half a mile of Burns's house at Ellisland, the Cumberland mountains may be seen; and since the days of Drayton the Scottish Scruffel and the English Skiddaw have recognised each other in popular verse. Wordsworth himself, on visiting the land of Burns, called this fact to mind :—

> " Huge Criffel's hoary top ascends,
>   By Skiddaw seen,—
> Neighbours we were, and loving friends
>   We might have been."

When Burns died, at the age of thirty-seven, Wordsworth was a young man of twenty-six. He had been destined for the Church, and with that view had gone to St. John's College, Cambridge, and taken his degree ;

but, caught as he had been from the first by the new spirit of song, then hanging most powerfully, as it would seem, over both shores of the Solway, he had already recognised his proper office, and consecrated his life to the Muses. In 1793, the year of the publication by Burns of the fourth edition of his Poems, Wordsworth had given to the world his first productions—two poems in the heroic couplet, entitled, respectively, *An Evening Walk, addressed to a Young Lady*, and *Descriptive Sketches, taken during a pedestrian Tour among the Alps*. These two compositions are slender enough; but how powerful was the impression that they produced on some minds by the peculiarity of their style may be inferred from the following testimony of another youthful poet, who, coming to Cambridge immediately after Wordsworth had left it, naturally took an interest in what his predecessor had done. " During the last year of my residence at Cambridge," says Coleridge, " I became acquainted with Mr. Wordsworth's first publication, entitled *Descriptive Sketches;* and seldom, if ever, was the emergence of an original poetic genius above the literary horizon more evidently announced." It was not till 1796, however, that the two poets became personally known to each other. Like Coleridge, Wordsworth, who had travelled, and resided in France during the fervours of the French Revolution, partook, and in no moderate degree, of the social enthusiasm of the time; and, the two aspirants having gone to live together for a summer in a pleasant retreat on the coast of Somersetshire, their demeanour, as Coleridge informs us in his *Biographia Literaria,* attracted so much local attention that Government was induced to send a spy to watch them. The poor man, however, after dogging them for some weeks in their walks, acquitted them of any disloyal intention, and even became ashamed of his office, feeling sure, as he said, from their continual talking of one *Spy-Nosy,* as they sat together for hours on a sandbank, behind which he lay concealed, that they had detected him, and were making game of him. As Wordsworth's tempo-rary sympathies with the French Revolution may be supposed to have placed him in vital connexion with one of the two great phenomena in which the sudden access of new energy to the human race at that time declared itself, so, we may also suppose, those sea-side conversations of his about *Spy-Nosy* with the " notice-able man with large grey eyes " must have placed him in sufficient connexion with the other pheno-menon, the Transcendental Philosophy. Moreover, in 1798, the two friends made a tour together in Germany; and whatever speculative insight was obtained by Coleridge during his whole life was evidently communicated, if not in the form of creed,

at least in the form of conception, to the less analytic
poet.

In 1798 Wordsworth published his *Lyrical Ballads ;*
to the second edition of which, printed in 1800, he
appended his first prose exposition of those principles
on which he professed to write, and to which Coleridge,
by the fact of his association with him in the publication (the *Ancient Mariner* appeared in companion-
ship with the *Lyrical Ballads*), virtually gave in his
adhesion.   Wordsworth's next publication was in 1807,
when he printed in two volumes a variety of poems
composed in preceding years.   Meanwhile he had
married, and had retired to his native Lakes, to lead
among their quiet beauties the tranquil life he deemed
alone suitable to the poetic nature.   Southey's subsequent retirement to the same part of the country,
and Coleridge's frequent visits to it, gave occasion
to the celebrated nickname of the " Lake School,"
applied to the three poets and their followers. With the
exception of a few tours in Scotland and the Continent, and occasional journeys to London, the whole
remainder of Wordsworth's long life was spent among
the Lakes.   Here, in the enjoyment of worldly compe-
tence, he walked, boated, wrote, and attended church ;
hence from time to time he issued his new poems, or
collections of poems, accompanied by prefaces or dissertations intended to illustrate their peculiar character ;

and here, in the bosom of his admiring family, he
received the chance visits of such stray worshippers as
came privileged with letters of introduction, talking
with them in a cold stately way, and not unfrequently
(be the truth distinctly spoken) shocking them by the
apparent egotism with which he referred to or quoted
his own poetry, the inordinate indifference he displayed
towards most things besides, the painful rigour with
which he exacted from those around him every outward
mark of respect and attention, and the seriousness with
which he would repeat the most insignificant words
that had been uttered in his praise. These particulars
regarding the man are already irrevocably before the
public in our books of literary gossip, and may not,
therefore, be wholly omitted even in a notice dedicated
to the poet. But, whatever may have been his bearing
in the presence of other men, Wordsworth was modest
and cordial in his communion with Nature. And it is
thus that we should remember him: not as the pleasant
ornament of the social board, lavishing the kind word
and the hearty repartee; not as the self-forgetting
enthusiast of the hour, burning his way through crowds,
and drawing adoration and love in his train; but as he
was in his old age, the conscious patriarch of English
poesy, the grey-haired and hard-featured recluse, shun-
ning the haunts of men, yet with a benevolent hand
for the familiar woes of the neighbourhood which knew

and honoured him, accustomed to walk alone by day
amid the woods, to pace muttering by the ripple of a
lake in the moonlight, or, standing half way up a
mountain, to turn his unearthly eye towards the heaven
of stars. Such he was through all the turmoil of a
generation into which, almost alone of his coevals, he
had lived to advance; and such he was till, in his
eighty-first year, death took him.

The nature of the revolution effected by Wordsworth
in the state of English poetry will be best understood
by attending to the exact tenor of certain propositions
advanced and illustrated by him in his various Prefaces
and Dissertations between 1800 and 1820. On these
propositions, as supplementary to his general critical
onslaught on the poetry of the previous age, he may be
supposed to have rested his claims to be considered not
only a poet, but also the father of a new poetical era.

Poetry, according to Wordsworth, "takes its origin
from emotion recollected in tranquillity:" what the poet
chiefly does, or ought to do, is to represent, out of real
life, scenes and passions of an affecting or exciting
character. Now, men originally placed in such scenes
use a nervous and exquisite language, expressly adapted
for the occasion by Nature herself; and the poet,
therefore, in imitating such scenes or passions, will
recall them more vividly in proportion as he can

succeed in employing the same language. Only one consideration should operate to make him modify that language : the consideration, namely, that his business as a poet is to give pleasure. All such words or expressions, therefore, as, though natural in the original transaction of a passionate scene, would be unpleasant in its poetic rehearsal, must be omitted. Pruned and weeded in accordance with this negative rule, any description of a moving occurrence, whether in prose or verse, would be true poetry. But, to secure still more perfectly their great end of giving pleasure while they excite emotion, poets have devised the artificial assistance of metre or verse. The *rationale* of the use of metre consists in this, that it provides for the reader or hearer a succession of minute pleasurable surprises, apart from, and independent of, the emotion produced by the matter for which it is the vehicle. A prose version of a passionate story, though, if well managed, it would not be so painful as the original transaction, and might even be pleasurable, would still in many cases be sufficiently painful to prevent its being read more than once. But, by narrating the same in metre, the poet is able, as it were, cunningly to administer a series of doses of pleasure, artificially prepared, which, though not very perceptible, are still sufficient, by mingling with the current of the meaning, to attemper and sweeten its effects. And rhyme is a still higher

form of the same device. The necessities, therefore, of
metre and rhyme do oblige certain departures in poetry
from the primary language of emotion; but, with
allowance for these, good poetic diction should still
approach very near to the language of real life.

This view, so useful as an attack upon the florid
diction of the poets of the preceding age, certainly errs
by exaggeration. Wordsworth's own poetry will not
stand to be tried by it; for, as Coleridge has shown,
there is hardly a verse, even in his most simple
productions, that does not deviate from the so-called
language of real life.   And it must inevitably be so.
For, in the first place, the mere application of the
negative principle of modification laid down by Wordsworth would amount to an abandonment of the point
at issue. Remove all that would be poetically unpleasant from the language of real passion in humble
life—the bad grammar, the incoherence, the mispro-
nunciations, and so on; and the language that would
then be left for the poet would be a very rare and
select language indeed, existing literally nowhere
throughout the community, but purely supposititious
and ideal, the sap and flower of all popular expression.
So also with the representation of passions of a higher
order.   The only sense in which the language of a
great part of our best poetry can be said to resemble
real language is that it is the kind of language that

a few of the most cultured persons of the community
would employ on very rare and impressive occasions.
But even the choicest spontaneous language of the
best minds when most nobly moved in real life must
undergo modification before it can be used by the
poet. And, though Wordsworth has provided for such
modification, by laying down the positive principle
that the poet is at all times to remember that it is
his office to give pleasure, and by pointing out the
operation of this principle as regards metre and rhyme,
yet he does not seem to have seen the whole energy
of this principle as determining and compelling departures from common usage. His argument for the
virtual identity of poetic language and the language
of real life reminds one of the mania for what is called
a simple conversational style. Why do not men write
as they speak? Why do they not convey their
meaning in books in the good racy English which
they employ at the dinner-table, or when giving their
household orders? Such are the absurd questions that
are asked every day. It never seems to enter into the
minds of these people that conversation is one thing,
public speaking another, and writing a third; that
each involves and requires a distinct setting of the
faculties for its exercise; that in passing from one to
either of the others certain powers must be called into
play that were before at rest, or sent to rest that were

before in play; and that, accordingly, to demand the
perpetual use of a conversational style is to insist that
there shall never be anything greater in the world
than what conversation can generate. But a world
thus restricted to the merely conversational method of
literary production would fall into decrepitude. When
a man talks with his friend, he is led on but by a
few trains of association, and finds a straggling style
natural for his purposes; when he speaks in public,
the wheels of thought glow, the associative processes
by which he advances become more complex, and hence
the roll, the cadence, the precipitous burst; and, lastly,
when he writes, still other conditions of thought come
into action, and there arises the elaborate sentence,
winding like a rivulet through the meadow of his
subject, or the page jewelled with a thousand allusions.
Precisely so in the matter more immediately under
discussion. Here, too, there is a gradation. A man
in a state of excitement talks in vivid language, and
even sets his words to a rough natural music, his voice
swelling or trembling with its burthen, though falling
short of song. But in the literary repetition of a
scene Nature suggests a new set of proprieties, answer-
ing to the entire difference between the mind in the
primary and the mind in the secondary attitude;
and a literal report would be found to defeat the
very end in view, and to be as much out of place

as a literal copy in painting. Even in prose narration there must be a more select and coherent
language than served in the primary act of passion,
as well as a more melodious music. And when, moved
to a still higher flight, the story lifts itself into
metre—availing itself of a device sanctioned by an
origin in some of the more splendid moments of the
ancient human soul—then, in exchange for certain
advantages, it submits to restrictions that come along
with them. Finally, if the charm of rhyme be desired,
this too must be purchased by farther and inevitable
concessions. Thus, we repeat, there is a gradation.
In prose narration language is conditioned by a more
complex set of necessities than in actual experience ;
in metrical narration the conditions are more complex
still, so that, if the speech were of marble before, there
must now be speech of jasper ; and, lastly, in rhyme
the conditions compel the thought through so fine a
passage that the words it chooses must be opals and
rubies. Nor in all this is there any departure from
nature. On the contrary, it is a fine provision that,
where the ordinary resources even of musical prose
are apt to fail, the mind should have more intense
methods of production in reserve. Such methods
are metre and rhyme. They do not impair the work
of intellectual invention, but rather assist it, and render
it capable of a more exquisite class of performances

than would otherwise be possible. In prose, however
musical, the meaning flows easily over a level, obeying
the guidance of its own associations; in metre new
associations are added, which, while they increase the
difficulty, also stimulate the intellect to higher reaches;
and, when with this is conjoined rhyme, or the obliga-
tion of conducting the already moving thought in the
direction or towards the horizon of a certain possible
number of preconceived sounds, then every fibre of
the mind is alert, the whole strength of the household is in action, and things are done that surprise the
gods.

Although there seems to be no doubt that the vehement opposition that greeted Wordsworth on his appearance as a poet was determined largely by a perception
on the part of the public of those weaknesses in his
theory to which we have been alluding, it seems plain
also that much of it was a mere display of that instinct
of indignation which seizes men when they see their
household deities attacked.

" ' Pedlars,' and ' boats,' and ' waggons !' Oh ! ye shades
    Of Pope and Dryden, are we come to this ? "

Such was the universal feeling of the critics. The
controversy between the *Edinburgh Review* and Wordsworth was literally a contest between the old and the
new; in which, however, the old derived certain advan-

tages from the obstinacy and want of tact with which
the new exposed and made a boast of its most galling
peculiarities. For, if Jeffrey's criticisms on Wordsworth's poetry be now compared with the criticisms
of Wordsworth's own friend Coleridge, as published
in the *Biographia Literaria,* it will be found that,
immeasurably as the two critics differ in spirit—
the one refusing to admit Wordsworth to be a good
poet at all, the other considering him to be the greatest
English poet since Milton—there is still an almost
perfect coincidence in their special objections to his
style. What Jeffrey attacked was chiefly the alleged
childishness of much of Wordsworth's language, the
babyism of his " Alice Fells," with their cloaks of
" duffle grey," &c.; and it is precisely on these points
that Coleridge, even while aware of his friend's more
profound reason for such familiarities, expresses his
dissent from him. The truth is, had Wordsworth been
a man of more innate energy, more tremendousness, as
a poet, he would have effected the revolution that was
necessary with less delay and opposition. Wrapping up
his doctrinal peculiarities, if he had had any, in the
midst of his poetry, instead of protruding them in a
preface, he would have blasted the old spirit out by
the mere infatuation of the new, and wound resistless
hands in the hair of the nation's instincts. But,
instead of being the Mirabeau of the literary revolu-

tion, hardly aware of his own propositions, he was, as it were, its Robespierre, who first threw his propositions tied in a bunch into the crowd before him, and then fought his way pertinaciously to where they fell. Even thus (and there were doubtless advantages in this method too) he at length obtained success. The "This will never do" with which Jeffrey introduced his criticism of the *Excursion* proved a false augury. Slowly and reluctantly the nation came round to Wordsworth; and, if there are still many that believe in his defects and shortcomings, all admit him to have been a true poet, and a man of rare genius. Of the poets that have appeared in England since he began his course—Byron, Shelley, Keats, Tennyson, and others—there is not one that does not owe something to his example and influence. Not that these men would not have been poets even had Wordsworth never lived. Through them, too, the new spirit would infallibly in any case have asserted itself; and, as it is, there has been in each of them something individual and original, which has caught portions of the new spirit that even the soul of Wordsworth did not, and been made capable thereby of perfectly specific work. A Nestor may be the patriarch of the camp, but even his deeds may be, in the end, outdone by the exploits of younger heroes. Of all the poets that have succeeded Wordsworth, the one who stands most in the position of revolt against him is Byron. The Byronic in poetry is, in some respects, the contradictory of the Wordsworthian. And believing that Byron was also a great poet, and that through him there were poured into our age elements of grandeur and power that were wanting in Wordsworth, and yet were needed, one would willingly go on to consider historically the appearance of this other tendency in our literature, known as the Byronic, and to show how the two tributaries became at length united. It is time, however, to leave the historical part of our subject, and direct our attention more expressly to the qualities of Wordsworth as a poet.

That Wordsworth was a true poet, that he did possess the "inherent glow," the "vision and faculty divine," no one that has ever read a page of his writings can honestly deny. Coleridge, in whose vocabulary the word "imagination" stood for the poetic faculty *par excellence*, pronounced Wordsworth to be, in imaginative power, "the nearest of all modern writers to Shakespeare and Milton." This estimate may be opposed by some as too high; but, if we keep in view the precise sense attached by Coleridge to his words, it will be difficult to lower it very much. Nor, in accepting such a judgment, is it necessary to have any profound theory as to the nature of this so-called imaginative or poetic faculty which we then assert him to possess. It is

sufficient if we know it when we see it, or if we feel
the force of any of those numerous synonyms and cir-
cumlocutions by which poets and analysts (Wordsworth
himself amongst others) have sought to describe it.
For, as some think, we define such terms best when we
rave about them, adhering to no one form of expression,
but supplementing the defects of all possible conception
by the vagueness and the force of sound.   Perhaps the
phrase which, if fully apprehended, would best convey
the notion of what is meant by imagination as the
faculty of the poet, would be the phrase "creative
energy."   For this phrase would carry with it one very
essential discrimination—the discrimination, namely,
of the poetic faculty, as such, both from that passive
sensibility by which the mind, presenting a photo-
graphic surface to the universe, receives from it
impressions of whatever is, and also from that minor
and more ordinary exercise of activity by which the
mind, sitting thereafter amid these received impressions,
recollects, registers, and compares them.   What the
imaginative or poetic faculty does is something beyond
this, and is more akin to the operation of that original
cosmic power at whose fiat the atoms and the elements sprang first together.   A certain accumulation
of material, a certain assemblage of impressions, or
mental objects, being supplied by the consciousness,
and lying there ready, it is the part of this faculty to

discharge **into** them a *self* that shall fuse them into **a**
living **whole,** capable of being contemplated with pleasure. **This—**the *poiesis* or creation of new unities, the
information of mere knowledge with somewhat of the
spirit of the knower, the incorporation of diverse impressions and recollections by the combining flash of a
specific mental act—is the function of the imagination.
Now, as all men possess this faculty in some degree,
and as in the generation of all the higher species of
thought or action it must be present in a very large
degree, by whatever names such species of thought
or action are called, it is only in a certain supreme sense
that imagination is set apart in all languages as the
proper faculty of poets. Yet there is reason in this.
Poets pre-eminently are men that breathe their own
spirit into things, that make self dominate over what is
distinct from self, that give out into the universe more
than they receive from it. So in Goethe's lines on the
poet—

" Wherewith bestirs he human spirits ?
　Wherewith makes he the elements obey ?
　Is't not the stream of song that out his bosom springs,
　And to his heart the world back coiling brings ? "

That is, the stream of song, or self, flowing forth from
the poet's heart into the world of phenomena, entwines
itself there with this and with that portion of matter

or experience, and then flows back to whence it came,
coiling what it has captured along with it.   This power,
this overflowing of self upon the universe, so characteristic of the poet, appears most of all in his eye.   The
eyes of some men are dull and obtuse ; those of others
are sharp and piercing, as if they shot their power out
in lines ; the eyes of the poet are heavy-laden and
melancholy, like pools continually too full.

However we may choose to vary the words that are
taken to define the essential faculty of the poet, we
shall find that they apply to Wordsworth.   Every page
of his poetry abounds with instances of imagination.
Thus, from the *Excursion*—

> " Some tall crag
> That is the eagle's birth-place, or *some peak*
> *Familiar with forgotten years*, that shows
> Inscribed upon its visionary sides
> The history of many a winter-storm,
> Or obscure record of the path of fire."

Or from *Peter Bell*—

> " And he had trudged through Yorkshire dales,
>   Among the rocks and winding scars ;
> Where deep and low *the hamlets lie*
> *Beneath their little patch of sky,*
>   *And little lot of stars.*"

Or from *Intimations of Immortality from Recollections
of Childhood*—

" Our birth is but a sleep and a forgetting :
　The Soul that rises with us, our life's star,
　　Hath had elsewhere its setting,
　　　And cometh from afar :
　　　Not in entire forgetfulness,
　　　And not in utter nakedness,
　But trailing clouds of glory do we come
　　　From God who is our home :
Heaven lies about us in our infancy !
Shades of the prison-house begin to close
　　　Upon the growing Boy ;
But he beholds the light, and whence it flows—
　　　He sees it in his joy ;
The Youth, who daily further from the east
　　Must travel, still is Nature's priest,
　　　And by the vision splendid
　　　Is on his way attended ;
At length the Man perceives it die away,
And fade into the light of common day."

These, and hundreds of other passages that might be
quoted, show that Wordsworth possessed, in a very high
degree indeed, the true primary quality of the poet—
imagination ; a surcharge of personality or vital spirit,
perpetually overflowing among the objects of the otherwise conditioned universe, and refashioning them according to its pleasure.

If we proceed now to inquire what were the most
prominent of those other characteristics which, acting
and re-acting with this generic tendency in the economy
of Wordsworth's mind, determined the specific pecu-

liarities of his poetical productions, we are sure to be impressed first of all by his extreme sensibility to, and accurate acquaintance with, the changing phenomena of external nature. It is a just complaint against civilization, as that word is at present defined, and especially against life in cities, that men are thereby shut out, or rather shut in, from sources of sensation the most pure and healthy of any. That people should know something of the aspects of the earth they live on; that they should be familiar with the features of at least a portion of its undisguised surface, with its rocks, its woods, its turf, its hills, as seen in the varying lights of day and night, and the varying livery of the seasons: this, it may be said, was clearly intended to be for ever a part of the mere privilege of existence. But a large proportion of mankind have been obliged to let slip even this poor item of their right in being. Pent up, on the one hand, in their cares against starvation, and, on the other, in their devices for artificial comfort, men have ceased to regard, with the same true intimacy as of old, the venerable face of their ancient mother. Certain great admonitions of the outward, indeed, will always remain with men wheresoever they pass their days—the overarching sky, the midnight winds, the sea's expanse, the yellow cornfield, the wooded landscape. And, after all, these are the images of nature that have most power to stir and affect us:

these, of which not even cities can deprive us. Cities, too, have their own peculiar kinds of scenery, of which, and especially of their nocturnal aspects, enough has not yet been made. Thus, in Keats's *Lamia*—

" As men talk in a dream, so Corinth all,
    Throughout her palaces imperial,
    And all her populous streets and temples lewd,
    Mutter'd, like tempest in the distance brew'd,
    To the wide-spreaded night above her towers."

But of the rural *minutiæ* of Nature, and also of what may be called her aspects of the horrible and lonesome, most of us, above all if we are denizens of cities, are compelled to be ignorant. . Very few, for example, can tell the names of the various forest trees, or distinguish them from each other; and fewer still can recognise, either by name or association, the various wild-flowers that grow in the meadows. How much also of sympathy with nature have we not lost by not knowing, with the shepherd or husbandman, the signs of the weather: what the clouds say when they hurry so, what mean those motions of the cattle, and why the mists roll down the hills? And then, in the more special region of phenomena to which we have referred, who among us experience, save by rare chance, the realities of those scenes so telling in books of fiction—the dark and solitary moor with the light glimmering in the distance, the fearful bivouac in the

depths of a wood, or the incessant breaking of the
waves at midnight against the cliff-embattled shore?

Now, it is a curious fact that one of the most characteristic features of that revolution in English
poetry with which the name of Wordsworth is associated has been the increased interest that it has both
instinctively aroused and knowingly cultivated in the
facts and appearances of material nature. If, as Wordsworth himself has said, hardly a new original image or
description of nature was introduced into English verse
in the age between Milton and Thomson, our recent
poets have certainly retrieved the neglect. "Nature,
nature," has been their cry; and as Bacon, after his
lordly fashion of thought, fancied that it was of service
to his health and spirits to inhale every morning the
smell of freshly-ploughed earth into which he had
poured wine, so they have interpreted literally their
prescriptions to the same effect, by renewing as often
as possible their acquaintance with the rural earth, and
falling periodically on the turf, as it were, with their
faces downwards. In particular, it must have been
remarked what an increased familiarity our recent
poets have contracted with the botanical department
of nature. Chaucer himself could hardly have described
the beauties of a field or a garden more minutely than
some of our modern versifiers. Nor among the poets
that have helped to cultivate this delight in the obser-

vation of natural appearances is there anyone that deserves to be ranked before Wordsworth. A native of scenes celebrated for their loveliness, he seems to have been endowed from the first with a capacity to feel and appreciate their benignant influence. In one of the few fragments that have been yet given to the world of his unpublished poem, *The Prelude,* he thus describes his sympathy with nature in childhood :—

>   " In November days,
> When vapours rolling down the valleys made
> A lonely scene more lonesome ; among woods
> At noon ; and 'mid the calm of summer nights,
> When, by the margin of the trembling lake,
> Beneath the gloomy hills, homeward I went
> In solitude, such intercourse was mine :
> Mine was it in the fields, both day and night,
> And by the waters, all the summer long.
> And in the frosty season, when the sun
> Was set, and, visible for many a mile,
> The cottage windows through the twilight blazed,
> I heeded not the summons : happy time
> It was indeed for all of us ; for me
> It was a time of rapture ! . . . Shod with steel
> We hissed along the polished ice, in games
> Confederate, imitative of the chase
> And woodland pleasures—the resounding horn,
> The pack loud chiming, and the hunted hare.
> So through the darkness and the cold we flew,
> And not a voice was idle : with the din
> Smitten, the precipices rang aloud ;

The leafless trees and every icy crag
Tinkled like iron ; while far distant hills
Into the tumult sent an alien sound
Of melancholy, not unnoticed, while the stars,
Eastward, were sparkling clear, and in the west
The orange sky of evening died away."

This intimacy with the face of the earth, this rich
and keen sense of pleasure in English nature, whether
in her vernal or her wintry aspects, Wordsworth carried
with him into manhood.   Submitting it, together with
all else that he knew of himself, to his judgment for
examination, he seems even to have arrived at a theory
that it is essential for every poet that would peacefully
possess his faculty in these modern times to connect
himself permanently and domestically with some appropriate spot or tract of scenery, the whole influence of
which he may thoroughly exhaust and incorporate with
his verse.   At least, in his own case, some such general
conviction · appears to have blended with the mere
sentiment of local attachment, which was doubtless
strong in him, in determining his retirement to the
Lakes.   There are even traces, we fancy, of a disposition on his part to generalize the feeling still more,
and to lay it down as a maxim that, in all ordinary
cases, the natal spot of every human being is the
appropriate spot of his activity through life, removal
from which must injure him, and that, so far as our

present social arrangements render this impossible, and
our present facilities for locomotion render the reverse
easy, so far we fall short of the ideal state of things.
In the abeyance of this law (hard law for many !)
lay, he seems to have felt, one of the great uses of
descriptive poetry.   While men do tear themselves
away from their native localities, and traverse the earth,
or congregate in cities, descriptive poetry, he persuaded
himself, must ever possess a refreshing and medicinal
virtue.   It was one of his most valued claims, therefore, that he should be considered a genuine English
descriptive poet.   And certainly this is a claim that
even those who think most humbly of his attainments
cannot deny him.   There would be a propriety, we
think, in remembering Wordsworth as a descriptive
poet along with Chaucer and Thomson, thus distinguishing him both from such poets as Burns and
Tennyson, on the one hand, and from such poets as
Keats on the other.   In such poets as Burns and
Tennyson, the element of what may be called *human
reference* is always so decided that, though no poets
describe nature more beautifully when they have occasion, it would still be improper to speak of them
specially as descriptive poets.   To borrow a distinction
from the sister art, it may be said that, if Burns and
Tennyson are more properly classed with the figure-
painters, notwithstanding the extreme beauty and finish

of their natural backgrounds, so, on the same principle, Wordsworth, whose skill in delineating the human subject is also admitted, may yet not erroneously be classed with the landscape-painters. On the other hand, he differs from poets like Keats in this, that, being a native of the country, and accustomed therefore to the appearances of rural nature in all seasons, he does not confound Nature with Vegetation. In the poetry of Keats, as all must feel, there is an excess of merely botanical imagery; in reading his descriptions we seem either to breathe the air of a hothouse, heavy with the moist odours of great-leafed exotics, or to lie full-stretched at noon in some shady nook in a wood, rank underneath with the pipy hemlock, and kindred plants of strange overgrowth. In Wordsworth, as we have seen, there is no such unhealthy lusciousness. He has his spots of thick herbage and his banks of florid richness too; but what he delights in is the broad, clear expanse, the placid lake, the pure pellucid air, the quiet outline of the mountain.

The second characteristic of Wordsworth's poetry to which we would call attention is the general intellectual vigour it displays, the large amount of really excellent thought that is bedded in it—thought that would have been valuable to the world in whatever form it had been put forth, and which might easily, had Wordsworth not been a poet, have been put forth otherwise than in metre. We have already asserted, with sufficient distinctness, that poetry is something essentially different from thought or proposition put into verse. A man may carry in his head a quantity of thought sufficient to set up a university, or to supersede a British Association, and yet be no poet. Or, on the other hand, a man may have something of the poetic spark in him, and be an intellectual weakling. It remains true, nevertheless, that intellect, or thought—clear, large intellect, such as would be available for any purpose whatever ; deep, abundant thought, such as we find in the best philosophical writings—is essential towards forming a great poet. This intellect of the poet may either exert itself in such a state of perfect diffusion through the rest of his mind in its creative act as only to become manifest in the completed grandeur of the result—which is the case, for example, with the poetry of Homer and Milton ; or it may retain its right to act also as a separate organ for the secretion of pure matter of thought—which is the case with the poetry of Shakespeare. In Wordsworth's poetry the presence of a superior intellect—an intellect strong, high, and subtle, if not of extreme dimensions —may be discovered by both of these tests. In the first place, the substance of his poetry, its logical compactness, and its entire freedom from mere commonplace, prove that a powerful and scholarly mind must

have presided over the work of production. On the
other hand, for proofs that Wordsworth was familiar,
even formally, with the best philosophical ideas of his
time, one needs only to dip into his *Excursion*, or any
other of his severer poems. Thus, in the following
passage, short as it is, the metaphysical reader will
discern a perfect mastery, on the part of the poet, over
a conception the power of grasping which is recognised
in the schools as the one test of a mind capable of
metaphysical studies:—

> " My voice proclaims
> How exquisitely the individual Mind
> (And the progressive powers perhaps no less
> Of the whole species) to the External world
> Is fitted :—and how exquisitely too—
> Theme this but little heard of among men—
> The External world is fitted to the Mind ;
> And the Creation (by no lower name
> Can it be called) which they with blended might
> Accomplish— this is our high argument."

This and similar conceptions of a very high metaphysics
were evidently as familiar to Wordsworth as they were
to Coleridge, from whom, it is very probable, he may
have originally derived some of them. Indeed, if we
make due allowance for the necessary difference
between the scientific and the poetic mode of presenting truths, it may be alleged that there is hardly

a notion of any generality put forth by Coleridge, whether in psychology, theology, politics, or literary criticism, some recognition of which may not be discovered either in the poems or in the prose dissertations of Wordsworth. The agreement between the two men intellectually seems to have been complete in almost every particular. Both professed political Conservatism; both conducted their speculative reasonings to a point where they merged in belief in Divine Revelation, and in a system of tenets derived from that belief, not differing essentially from theological orthodoxy; and both exhibited an ardent attachment to the forms and rules of the Church of England. It may even be questioned by a certain class of critics whether Wordsworth, in his treatment of such matters, has not sometimes taken leave of the poetical mood altogether, and assumed the mood of the preacher; whether the didactic fit did not sometimes overcome him in his poetry, and whether he has not allowed the controversial spirit, so manifest in his prefaces, to run over also somewhat deleteriously into his verse.

As distinct from the general intellectual excellence of Wordsworth's productions, we have to notice, farther, their singularly calm, religious, and contemplative tone. By thoughtfulness or contemplativeness we usually mean something quite distinguishable from mere intellectual vigour or opulence. The French are an intel-

E

lectual nation ; they think rapidly and powerfully ; but they do not answer to our notion of a thoughtful or contemplative people. Contemplativeness, according to our usage of the word, does not so much imply the power of attaining or producing thought as the power of brooding sentimentally over thought already attained. If we first oppose the speculative to the active, and then make a farther distinction between the speculative and the contemplative, the character of Hamlet in Shakespeare may be taken to represent the union of the speculative and the contemplative. The Prince is a student from the university, daring into all questions, and fertile at every moment in new generalities and pregnant forms of expression ; but his peculiarity consists in this, that far back in his mind there lie certain permanent thoughts and conceptions, towards which he always reverts when left alone, and from which he has ever to be roused afresh when anything is to be done. Now it is this tendency to relapse into a few favourite and constitutional trains of thought that makes the contemplative character. Nor is it difficult to see in what thought it is, above all others, that the contemplative mind will always find its most appropriate food. Birth, death, the future ; the sufferings and misdeeds of man in this life, and his hopes of a life to come ; the littleness of us and our whole sphere of knowledge, and the awful relations in which we stand

to a world of the supernatural—these, if any, are the
permanent and inevitable objects of human contemplation and solicitude. From age to age these thoughts
have been handed down; every age must entertain,
and no age can conclude, them. What the ancient
Chaldean meditated as he lay at night under the stars
of the desert, the same things does the modern
student meditate as he paces his lonely room. "Man,
that is born of woman, is of few days and full of
trouble;" "How can a man be justified with
God?" "O that one might plead for a man with
God as a man pleadeth for his neighbour!"—amid
all the changes of manners, dynasties, and races,
these thoughts survive. They, and such like, are
the peculiarly human thoughts, the thoughts of
humanity as such, the thoughts upon which mankind
must always fall back, and compared with which all
other thoughts are but intrusions and impertinences.
Now, although it would be possible to show that the
effect even of abstract speculation, if carried far enough,
is to lead men back into these thoughts and keep them
there, so that in this sense the most speculative men
must, as if by compulsion, become profoundly contemplative, yet for general purposes a distinction may be
drawn between men who are speculative and men who
are contemplative in their tendencies. Some men are
always active intellectually, always engaged in some

E 2

process of inquiry and ingenuity—inventing a machine, scheming a project, discovering a law of mind or matter. These men are, in the present sense, speculative men; they are continually at work *within* the ascertained sphere of human activity; and it is by the labours of such men that the mass of this world's experience of its own self-contained capabilities has been accumulated. But there are other men who, either without being mentally active in this way, or besides being thus active, have a constitutional tendency at all times to fall into a musing attitude, to relapse, as we have already expressed it, into certain ancient and footworn trains of thought that lead apparently nowhither. These are the contemplative men. They are the men whose favourite position is rather at the circumference of the known sphere than within it, the men who, at whatever time they may be born, receive, cherish, and transmit the permanent and characteristic thoughts of the human race. This quality of contemplativeness is always associated in our minds with the idea of sadness, tearfulness, melancholy. The patriarch Isaac, of whom we are told that he went out into the fields to meditate at eventide, seems, in our fancy, the most mild and pensive of the characters of Scripture. And such men are the salt of the earth. There may be little originality, indeed, in the thoughts that form the appropriate food of the contemplative mind. To realize the conception "All flesh is grass," or the conception "Why do the wicked prosper?" seems but a very small effort of the intellect, by no means comparable to the effort required in almost every act of daily life. Nevertheless, it remains true that it is only out of a deep soil of such old and simple conceptions that any kind of true human greatness can rear itself, and also that there are very few minds indeed, in these days of ours, over which these and similar conceptions have their due degree of power. It is accordingly one of the chief merits of Wordsworth that in him this reference to the supernatural, this disposition to interpret all that is visible in the spirit of a conviction of its evanescence, did exist in a very high and unusual measure. He was essentially a pensive or contemplative man, one who was perpetually recurring to those few extreme thoughts and conceptions which most men never care to reach, and beyond which no man can go. This, which was conspicuous in the very aspect of his countenance, and which his recluse life illustrated, he has himself explicitly asserted.

> " On man, on nature, and on human life,
>   Musing in solitude, I oft perceive
>   Fair trains of imagery before me rise,
>   Accompanied by feelings of delight
>   Pure, or with no unpleasing sadness mixed ;
>   And I am conscious of affecting thoughts
>   And dear remembrances, whose presence soothes

> Or elevates the mind, content to weigh
> The good and evil of our mortal state.
> To these emotions, whencesoe'er they come,
> Whether from breath of outward circumstance,
> Or from the soul—an impulse to herself—
> I would give utterance in numerous verse."

It is the blending in Wordsworth of this contemplative tendency with so much general vigour of intellect that has earned for him the name of the English Philosophical Poet. It ought to be observed, at the same time, that in all Wordsworth's contemplative poetry the influence of Christian doctrine is plainly discernible. His meditations on Man, Nature, and the Future, are not those of a Pagan sage, however his language may sometimes consist even with a lofty Pagan view of the universe: on the contrary, he seems to think throughout as one in whose manner of transacting those great and paramount conceptions that form the necessary matter of all real contemplation that sweet modification had been wrought which Christianity has rendered possible.

One of the results of Wordsworth's naturally pensive disposition, left to expatiate as it chiefly was among the objects of a retired and pastoral neighbourhood, was that it gave him a specially keen and sympathetic eye for the characteristic miseries of rural life. We do not think that he was the man that could

> "hang
> Brooding above the fierce confederate storm
> Of sorrow barricadoed evermore
> Within the walls of cities;"

but no man better than he could

> "hear Humanity in fields and groves
> Pipe solitary anguish."

In pathetic stories of humble rural life we know no poet superior to Wordsworth. All the ordinary and, if we may so speak, parochial woes of rural existence in England seem to have been diligently noted and pondered by him. It is told of Burns by Dugald Stewart that, as they were walking together one morning in the direction of the Braid Hills, near Edinburgh, where they commanded a prospect of the adjacent country, the poet remarked that the sight of so many smoking cottages gave a pleasure to his mind which he did not believe anyone could understand that did not know, as he did, how much of real worth and happiness such poor habitations might contain. Now, if the glance with which Wordsworth, in his poetry, looks abroad on the cottage-sprinkled scenery of his native district cannot be said to show that warm familiarity with the daily tenor of humble rustic life which Burns had from experience, it may at least be compared to the kindly glance of some pious and diligent pastor, such as Wordsworth has himself described in his *Excursion*, surveying from a height the scattered homes of his well-known parishioners. At home in the parsonage there are books, pictures, and a piano, the care of a gentle wife or daughters; in walking over the fields, too, the pastor, an academic and cultured man, has necessarily thoughts and enjoyments of his own; nevertheless, what he has seen and known of the habits of those among whom he labours has given him an eye to perceive, and a heart to appreciate, their lowliest anxieties and sorrows. Almost exactly so it is with Wordsworth. The incidents of rural life that he delights to depict are precisely those that would arouse the interest and occupy the attention of some good clergyman, active in his duties, and accustomed to store up in his memory the instructive annals of his parish. The death of a poor seduced girl, the return of a disabled soldier to his native village, the wreck of the fortunes of a once thriving family, the solitude of aged widowhood, the nightly moanings of a red-cloaked maniac haunting some dreary spot in the woods— nothing can exceed the pathos with which Wordsworth can tell such simple local stories as these. One can hardly read without tears some of his narratives of this kind: for example, the poem entitled *Guilt and Sorrow*, the pastoral entitled *Michael*, or the tale of the widow Margaret and her lonely cottage as told in the

first book of the *Excursion.* Showing a similar eye for
the moral picturesque in humble rural life, though altogether of a more cheerful character, is the hearty tale
of the *Waggoner,* perhaps one of the most perfect of
all Wordsworth's compositions. And here we may
remark that, if Wordsworth had any such theory as
we have supposed as to the advantage, in the poetical
occupation, of a permanent connexion of the poet with
some one spot or district, then, in such a theory, he
must necessarily have had respect as well to the power
of familiar modes of life to form the heart of the poet as
to the influence of familiar scenery in attuning his
imagination. And certainly there is much in this.
Rarely does one that has removed from his native spot
form elsewhere relations that can stand him in stead
when he wishes to glance into human life at once
intimately and broadly.

Somewhat dissociated in appearance from those
characteristics of Wordsworth which we have already
mentioned, but demonstrably compatible with them,
was his strong sense of the antique: his lively interest
in the traditional, the legendary, and the historical. We
see in Wordsworth, in this respect, a certain similarity
to a man from whom otherwise he differed much—
Sir Walter Scott. The English poet seems to have had
the same liking for significant anecdotes and snatches
of ancient song and ballad, the same reverence for

pedigree, and the same pleasure in associating places known to him with celebrated transactions of the past, as were observable, in still larger degree, in the Scottish novelist. Among the poems that exemplify this characteristic of our author are the dramatic poem of *The Borderers*, the beautiful poem entitled *Hart-leap Well*, the long legendary poem of *The White Doe of Rylstone* (which is in the metre, and somewhat in the style, of much of Scott's poetry), and also many of the shorter pieces written during tours in Scotland and in various parts of England. A particular illustration of this quality of Wordsworth's mind is also presented in his Scott-like habit of introducing, almost lovingly, topographical references and the names of places into his verse. Thus, in the poem *To Joanna*, describing the echo of a lady's laugh heard among the mountains :—

> " The rock, like something starting from a sleep,
> Took up the Lady's voice, and laughed again ;
> That ancient woman seated on Helm-crag
> Was ready with her cavern ; Hammar-scar
> And the tall steep of Silverhow sent forth
> A noise of laughter ; Southern Loughrigg heard,
> And Fairfield answered with a mountain tone ;
> Helvellyn far into the clear blue sky
> Carried the Lady's voice ; old Skiddaw blew
> His speaking-trumpet ; back out of the clouds
> Of Glaramara southward came the voice ;
> And Kirkstone tossed it from his misty head."

But most conspicuously of all the poet has exhibited his interest in the antique and historical, and his power of imaginatively reproducing it, in his fine series of Ecclesiastical Sonnets, wherein he traces, as in a series of bold retrospective glimpses, the history of Christianity in the British Islands. There are passages in these Sonnets worth, for historical effect, many pages of the writings of our ecclesiastical historians.

Of the various other excellences of Wordsworth we will particularize but one more—the exquisite propriety and delicacy of his style, his easy and perfect mastery over the element of language. He must have possessed a natural gift of rich and exuberant expression; but it is equally evident that he must have, at a very early period, submitted this natural exuberance to a careful and classic training, and also that he must have bestowed his best pains in finishing, according to his own ideas of correctness, all his compositions individually. Hence greater smoothness and beauty, and more of strict logical coherence, in Wordsworth's style than is usual even among careful poets, as well as a more close fitting of the language to the measure of the thought, and a comparative freedom from forced rhymes and jarring evasions of natural forms of words. This appears even in the greater typographical neatness of a printed page of Wordsworth's poetry, as compared, for example, with a printed page of Byron's, the lax and

dash-disrupted look of which suggests to practised eyes
the notion at once of more energetic genius and greater
literary haste.   Specimens of Wordsworth's extreme
felicity of expression have already been given in the
previous extracts ; and in selecting for incessant repetition such poems of his as *We are Seven,* and such
lines as those famous ones about the " yellow primrose,"
the public have already indicated their appreciation in
his case of this merit in particular.   A quotation or
two, however, illustrative of the same thing, may here
be added.   Observe how variously and yet simply the
language, in the following passages, pursues the intri-
cacies and adapts itself to the mood of the meaning :—

" A village churchyard, lying as it does in the lap of
Nature, may indeed be most favourably contrasted with
that of a town of crowded population ; and sepulture
therein combines many of the best tendencies which
belong to the mode practised by the ancients with
others peculiar to itself.   The sensations of pious
cheerfulness which attend the celebration of the
Sabbath-day in rural places are profitably chastised by
the sight of the graves of kindred and friends, gathered
together in that general home towards which the thoughtful yet happy spectators themselves are journeying.
Hence, a parish church, in the stillness of the country,
is a visible centre of a community of the living and the
dead, a point to which are habitually referred the
nearest concerns of both."—*Essay on Epitaphs.*

" To all that binds the soul in powerless trance,
Lip-dewing song, and ringlet-tossing dance."
Descriptive Sketches.

" She dwelt among the untrodden ways
  Beside the springs of Dove,
A maid whom there were none to praise,
  And very few to love :
A violet by a mossy stone
  Half hidden from the eye !
Fair as a star when only one
  Is shining in the sky !
She lived unknown, and few could know
  When Lucy ceased to be ;
But she is in her grave, and, oh,
  The difference to me ! "
Miscellaneous Poems.

" Then up I rose,
And dragged to earth both branch and bough, with crash
And merciless ravage ; and the shady nook
Of hazels, and the green and mossy bower,
Deformed and sullied, patiently gave up
Their quiet being : and, unless I now
Confound my present feelings with the past,
Ere from the mutilated bower I turned
Exulting, rich beyond the wealth of kings,
I felt a sense of pain when I beheld
The silent trees, and saw the intruding sky."
Nutting.

" Great God ! I'd rather be
A pagan suckled in a creed outworn ;
So might I, standing on this pleasant lea,

Have glimpses that would make me less forlorn ;
Have sight of Proteus rising from the sea ;
Or hear old Triton blow his wreathèd horn."

Sonnets.

"Nuns fret not at their convent's narrow room ;
And hermits are contented with their cells ;
And students with their pensive citadels ;
Maids at the wheel, the weaver at his loom,
Sit blithe and happy ; bees that soar for bloom
High as the highest peak of Furness-fells
Will murmur by the hour in foxglove bells :
In truth, the prison unto which we doom
Ourselves no prison is : and hence to me,
In sundry moods, 'twas pastime to be bound
Within the Sonnet's scanty plot of ground ;
Pleased if some souls (for such there needs must be)
Who have felt the weight of too much liberty
Should find brief solace there, as I have found."

Sonnets.

That we would assign to Wordsworth a high place
among the poets of England the whole tenor of our
observations hitherto will have made clear. At the
same time, that he falls short of the very highest rank,
that he does not stand on the very top of our English
Parnassus, where Chaucer, Milton, and Spenser keep
reverent company with Shakespeare, but rather on that
upper slope of the mountain whence these greatest are
visible, and where various other poets hold perhaps as
just, if not so fixed, a footing : this also we have sought

to convey as part of our general impression. We do not think, for example, that Wordsworth was so great a poet as Burns; and, if it is only in respect of general mental vigour and capacity, and not in respect of poetic genius *per se*, that Dryden, Pope, and Coleridge, could be justly put in comparison with Wordsworth, and, being so put in comparison, preferred to him on the whole, yet there are others in our list of poets for whom, even after the ground of competition has been thus restricted, we believe it would be possible to take up the quarrel. With all the faults of Byron, both moral and literary, the poetic efflux in *him* came from greater constitutional depths, and brought, if less pure, at least more fervent, matter with it than the poetry of Wordsworth: had Keàts and Shelley lived longer, even those that sneer at the Byronic might have seen poets comparable, in their estimation, to the Patriarch of the Lakes; and, should our noble Tennyson survive as a constant writer till his black locks have grown grey, one sees qualities in him that predict for him more than a Wordsworth's fame. Keeping in view, therefore, these comparisons and contrasts, it seems proper that we should add to the foregoing enumeration of some of Wordsworth's characteristic excellences a word or two descriptive of some accompanying defects.

First of all, then, as it seems to us, the intellect of Wordsworth, though very far beyond the ordinary in its dimensions, and very assiduously developed by culture, was by no means of the largest known English calibre. Not to bring into the comparison such rare giants as Shakespeare, Bacon, and Milton, there have been, and probably still are, very many distinguished men in our island fit to rank intellectually as the peers of Wordsworth, or even as his superiors. Making the necessary discrimination between native intellectual strength to arrive at conclusions and the soundness of the conclusions arrived at, one would say that Johnson, Burke, Burns, David Hume, and not a few others that might be named, were presumably men of more powerful intellect than Wordsworth. Partly because of the time at which they lived, partly from causes for which they were personally more responsible, the intellectual conclusions of those men, or of some of them, may have been less noble and lofty than those of Wordsworth, their favourite forms of thought more coarse, their philosophy less true, deep, and ethereal. But their intellectual strength or grasp, their sense and insight, their whole available power to do, discern, and invent, were perhaps greater. Even of Pope, on whose reputation as a poet Wordsworth and his followers have been so severe, it might be maintained that, comparison of poetic merit apart, his was the denser and nimbler brain. Nor would the greatest admirers of Wordsworth say that in force and reach of intellect he excelled his friend Coleridge. Fine, stately, and silvery as Wordsworth's prose writings are, they want the depth, originality, and richness of the similar compositions of that old man eloquent. Wordsworth's, in short, was not a vast or prodigious, but only a very high and serene intellect. Now, though it has been already shown that it is not intellect as such that makes a poet, but that either a man may have a great intellect and be no poet or may be a poet without having an extraordinary intellect, yet, as it has been shown also that to constitute a great poet great intellect is essential, we may assume it as a fact that the measure of the general intellectual power of any particular poet is also so far a measure of his poetic excellence. According to this rule, we should first apply the intellectual test, so as to decide Wordsworth's place (probably beside such men as Coleridge and Dryden) in our general hierarchy of English men of letters of all sorts taken together; then, dividing this miscellaneous body into kinds or classes, we should retain Wordsworth exactly at his ascertained height among the poets; and, lastly, allowing to the whole class of poets as much additional elevation as might be thought necessary, on the score of any supposed superiority of the poetical constitution as such, we should fix Wordsworth's just place among all the ornaments of English literature.

A second defect in Wordsworth is his want of

humour. This charge has been made so often against other celebrated writers that one is almost ashamed to bring it forward again in any new case whatever. Nevertheless, it is a charge of real weight against any one regarding whom it can be proved, and it is hardly necessary to offer proofs that it is true regarding Wordsworth. There are, indeed, poems of his, such as *The Waggoner, The Idiot Boy*, and *The Street Musician*, that display a kind of genial and warm interest in the little pleasant blunders and less than tragic mishaps of daily life; but in such instances we seem to recognise the air of the poet as that of a sedate dreamer looking at matters, or hearing of them, with a hard benevolent smile, rather than as that of a man of hearty native humour, recklessly enjoying what is jocose. There is no real mirth, no rich sense of the comic, in all that Wordsworth has written. In that full sly love of a jest that lurks in the down-looking eye of Chaucer, as well as in the broad and manly capacity of laughter that distinguished Burns, the poet of the Lakes was totally wanting. Hence it is that, among all his characters, he has given us none like the Host of the Tabard in the *Canterbury Pilgrimage*, and that, living as he did in a notable part of England, the whole spirit and peculiarity of which he sought to make his own, he could not imbibe or reproduce its humours. Whenever, in obedience to an intellectual perception of the existence in society of such so-called " humours," he attempts to introduce them into his poetry, he either only reaches the playful, or betrays his natural seriousness by keeping the moral lesson strictly in view. Now, though there have been really great poets, Milton and Schiller for example, in whom this defect of humour was as marked as in Wordsworth, yet in such cases it will be found that the defect did, after all, operate to some extent injuriously, and had to be made good in some way by very ample compensations. If Milton had not humour, he had a large measure of what may properly enough be called wit, an infinite power of scorn, and a tremendous mastery of the language of abuse and sarcasm. As regards Byron, also, not to mention Pope, it is impossible to say how much not only of his popularity, but also of his real worth as a poet, may depend on the quantity of admirable wit which he brought into the service of the Muse. But in Wordsworth there is almost as little of wit, properly so called, as of humour. His moods are a benevolent seriousness, a rapt and spiritual state of the feelings, and a mild and sacerdotal sympathy with all that he sees. He may feel contempt, as indeed few men are said to have done in a greater degree, but he has no art in the ludicrous expression of it; he sometimes smiles, but he never laughs. In a poet of actual English life this is to be regarded as a considerable disqualification.

F 2

We may indicate another deficiency in Wordsworth by repeating the common criticism that he lacks energy, fire, impulse, intensity, passion. Wordsworth was, according to his own definition of a poet, " a man endowed with more lively sensibility, more enthusiasm and tenderness, than are supposed to be common among mankind ; " but what we now mean is something quite consistent with this. There was no tremendousness, nothing of the Pythic, in the nature of Wordsworth.

> " I surely not a man ungently made,"

are the fitting words he uses in describing himself. A calm, white-haired sage, who could thrill to the beauty of a starry night, and not a swart-faced Titan like Burns, full of strength and fire, was the poet of the *Excursion.* With all his pathos, all his clearness of vision, there were sorrows of humanity he never touched, recesses of dark moral experience he could not pierce nor irradiate. We feel in his poetry as if we were spoken to by some mild and persuasive preacher, rather than borne down by the experienced utterance of a large-hearted man. He does not move us to the depths of our being ; he only affects us gently. One reason for this must be that, naturally and by birth, Wordsworth was deficient in some of the more formidable elements of the human constitution. Possessing in large degree the elements of intellect, sensibility, and imagination, he seems to have been wanting in the Byronic element of personal passion. Moreover, and partly in consequence of this, he appears to have passed through the battle of life all but unwounded. This of itself would account for the placid, self-possessed, and often feeble style of his poetry. In the life of every man distinguished for what is called momentum of character there will almost certainly be found some sore biographical circumstance —some fact deeper and more momentous than all the rest—some strictly historical source of melancholy, that must be discovered and investigated if we would comprehend his ways. Man comes into this world regardless and unformed; and, although in his gradual progress through it he necessarily acquires, by the mere use of his senses and by communication with others, a multitudinous store of impressions and convictions, yet, if there is to be anything specific and original in his life, this, it would seem, can only be produced by the operation upon him of some one overbearing accident or event, which, rousing him to new wakefulness, and evoking all that is latent in his nature, shall bind these impressions and convictions in a mass together, breathe through them the sternness of personal concern, and impart to them its seal and pressure. The experiences that most commonly perform this function in the lives of men are those of Friendship and Love. The power of Love to rouse men to larger and more fervid views of nature has been celebrated since the beginning of time. A man that has once undergone Love's sorrow in any extreme degree is by that fact awakened at once and for ever to the melancholy side of things; he becomes alive to the gloomy in nature and to the miserable in life; and, by one stupendous resumption of stars, clouds, trees, and flowers, into his own pained being, like an old coinage requiring re-issue, he realizes how it is that all creation groaneth and travaileth together in spirit until now. So also, though perhaps more rarely, with the influence of exalted and lost Friendship. But Wordsworth, happily for himself, seems to have met with no such accident of revolution. Passing through the world as a pilgrim, pure-minded, and even sad with the sense of the mysterious future, nothing occurred in his journey to strike him down as a dead man, and agonize him into a full knowledge of the whole mystery of the present. Hence, we believe, the want of that intensity in his poetry which we find in the writings, not only of the so-called subjective poets, such as Byron and Dante, but also of the greatest objective poets, as Goethe and Shakespeare. The ink of Wordsworth is rarely his own blood.

It is little more than an extension of the last remark

to say that Wordsworth was rather a poet or bard than
(if we may be allowed the distinction) a lyrist or
minstrel. The purpose of the poet, to use the term
for the moment in this restricted sense, is to describe,
narrate, or represent some portion of the external, as it
is rounded out and made significant in his own mind ;
the purpose of the lyrist or minstrel is to pour forth
the passing emotions of his soul and inflame other men
with the fire that consumes himself. Accordingly, the
faculties most special to the merely poetic exercise,
as in the old Homeric epos or in modern descriptive
verse, are those of intellect, sensibility, and imagination
—passion or personal excitement being but a separate
element, which may be more or less present according
to circumstances, and which ought, as some think, to be
absent from pure poetry altogether ; whereas, in lyrical
effusion, on the other hand, passion or present excitement is nearly all in all. The poetry of Keats may be
taken as a specimen of pure poetry as such : all his
chief poems are literally *compositions* or creations, the
results of a process by which the poet's mind, having
projected itself into an entirely imaginary element,
devoid of all connexion with the present, worked and
moved therein slowly and fantastically at its own will
and pleasure. As specimens, again, of the purely
lyrical, we have all such pieces, ancient and modern, as

are properly denominated psalms, odes, hymns, or
songs. When, therefore, people talk, as they now incessantly do, of calmness as being essential to the poet,
and when, with Wordsworth, they define the poetic art
to consist in the tranquil recollection of bygone emotion,
it is clear that they can have in view only pure poetry,
the end of which is to represent in an imaginative manner some portion of the outward. For, of the lyrist
or song-writer it may be affirmed, just as of his near
kinsman the orator, that the more of passion or personal impetus he has the better; and, so far from
advising him to wait for complete tranquillity, one
would advise him to select, as the true lyrical moment,
that first moment, whenever it is, when the primary
perturbation has just so far subsided that his trembling
hands can sweep the strings. But with this difference
comes another. The poet, in describing his scene or
narrating his story, feels himself impelled to every
legitimate mode of increasing the pleasure he conveys ;
and the result, in one direction, is Metre. But, however natural Metre may have been in its origin, it has
now become to the poet rather a pre-established arrangement or available set of conditions, to the rule of
which he adapts what he has already in other respects
rendered complete, than a compulsory suggestion of the
poetic act itself. Not so with the lyrist. As cadence

or musical utterance is natural in an excited state of
the feelings, so in lyrical poetry ought the song or
melody to be more than the words. The heart of the
lyrist should be a perpetual fountain of song; and,
when he is to hold direct communication with the
world, an inarticulate hum or murmur, rising, as it
were, from the depths of his being, ought to precede
and necessitate all the actual speech. Now, in this
lyrical capability, this love of sound or cadence for its
own sake, Wordsworth is certainly inferior to many
other poets. One might have inferred as much from
the narrowness of his theory of verse; but the fact is
rendered still more apparent by a perusal of his poems
themselves. Very few poets have been more admirable
masters of poetic metre : no versification is more clear,
various, and flexible, or more soothing to the ear, than
that of Wordsworth. But he is not a singer or a minstrel properly so called; the lyric madness does not
seize him; verse with him is rather an exquisite
variety of rhetoric, a legitimate æsthetic device, than
a necessary form of utterance. Seldom in Wordsworth
is there a stanza after reading which and quite losing
sight of the words we are still haunted (as we constantly are in Burns, Byron, and Tennyson) by an
obstinate recollection of the tune. Were we required
to say in what portion of Wordsworth's poetry he has

shown most of this true lyric spirit, in which we believe him to have been on the whole deficient, we should unhesitatingly mention his Sonnets. These are among the finest and most sonorous things in our language ; and it is by them, in conjunction with his *Excursion* (or, as we may now say, *The Recluse*) that his great name will be most surely perpetuated.

II.

SCOTTISH INFLUENCE IN BRITISH LITERATURE.

II.

SCOTTISH INFLUENCE IN BRITISH LITERATURE.[1]

IT was in the winter of 1786-87 that the poet Burns, a
new prospect having been suddenly opened up to him
by the kind intervention of Blacklock and a few other
influential men in Edinburgh, abandoned his desperate
project of emigrating to the West Indies, and hastened
to pay his memorable first visit to the Scottish metro-
polis. During that winter, as all who are acquainted
with his life know, the Ayrshire ploughman, then in his
twenty-ninth year, was the lion of Edinburgh society.
Lord Monboddo, Dugald Stewart, Harry Erskine, Dr.
Robertson, Dr. Hugh Blair, Henry Mackenzie, Dr.
Gregory, Dr. Black, Dr. Adam Ferguson: such were
the names then most conspicuous in the literary capital

---

[1] *North British Review*, August 1852.—"Life of Lord Jeffrey: with
a Selection from his Correspondence." By Lord COCKBURN, one of the
Judges of the Court of Session in Scotland. **2** vols. 1852. [What
is here printed is only the introductory part of the article as it stood
in the *Review.*]

of North Britain ; and it was in the company of these
men, alternated with that of the Creeches, the Smellies,
the Willie Nicols, and other contemporary Edinburgh
celebrities of a lower grade, that Burns first realized
the fact that he was no mere bard of local note, but
a new power and magnate in Scottish Literature.

To those who are alive to the poetry of coincidences
two anecdotes connected with this residence of Burns
in Edinburgh will always be interesting.

What reader of Lockhart's *Life of Scott* has ever forgotten the account there given of Scott's first and only
interview with Burns ? As the story is now more
minutely told in Mr. Robert Chambers's *Life of Burns,*
Scott, who was then a lad of sixteen, just removed from
the High School to a desk in his father's office, was
invited by his friend and companion, the son of Dr.
Ferguson, to accompany him to *his* father's house on
an evening when Burns was to be there. The two
youngsters entered the room, sat down unnoticed by
their seniors, and looked on and listened in modest
silence. Burns, when he came in, seemed a little out
of his element. Instead of mingling at once with the
company, he kept going about the room, looking at the
pictures on the walls. One print particularly arrested
his attention. It represented a soldier lying dead
among the snow, his dog on one side, and a woman
with a child in her arms on the other. Underneath

the print were some lines of verse descriptive of the subject, which Burns read aloud with a voice faltering with emotion. A little while after, turning to the company and pointing to the print, he asked if any one could tell him who was the author of the lines. No one chanced to know, except Scott, who remembered that they were from an obscure poem of Langhorne's. The information, whispered by Scott to some one near, was repeated to Burns; who, after asking a little more about the matter, rewarded his young informant with a look of kindly interest, and the words, (Sir Adam Ferguson reports them,) "You'll be a man yet, sir." Such is the story of the "literary ordination," as Mr. Chambers well calls it, of Scott by Burns. It is a scene which Sir William Allan should have been the man to paint.

The other story is now told for the first time by Lord Cockburn. Somewhere about the very day on which the foregoing incident happened, "a little black creature" of a boy, we are told, who was going up the High Street of Edinburgh, and staring diligently about him, was attracted by the appearance of a man whom he saw standing on the pavement. He was taking a leisurely view of the object of his curiosity, when some one standing at a shop-door tapped him on the shoulder, and said, "Ay, laddie, ye may weel look at that man! that's Robert Burns." The "little black creature," thus early addicted to criticism, was Francis Jeffrey, the junior of Scott by two years, and exactly four years behind him in the classes of the High School, where he was known as a clever nervous little fellow, who never lost a place without crying. It is mentioned by Lord Cockburn that Jeffrey's first teacher at the High School, a Mr. Luke Fraser, had the good fortune to send forth, from three successive classes of four years each, three pupils no less distinguished than Walter Scott, Francis Jeffrey, and Henry Brougham.

It is not for the mere purpose of anecdote that we cite these names and coincidences. We should like very much to make out for Scotland in general as suggestive a series of her intellectual representatives as Lord Cockburn has here made out for part of the pedagogic era of the worthy and long dead Mr. Luke Fraser. Nor is it a difficult task.

Confining our regards to the eighteenth century, the preceding paragraphs enable us to group together at least three conspicuous Scottish names as belonging, by right of birth, to the third quarter of that century— Burns, born in Ayrshire in 1759; Scott, born in Edinburgh in 1771; and Jeffrey, born in the same place in 1773. Suppose, however, that we go a little farther back for some other prominent Scottish names of the same century. Then the readiest to occur to the memory will be these:—James Thomson, the poet, born in Roxburghshire in 1700; Thomas Reid, the philosopher, born near Aberdeen in 1710; David Hume, born at Edinburgh in 1711; Robertson, the historian, born in Mid-Lothian in 1721; Tobias Smollett, the novelist, born at Cardross in the same year; Adam Smith, born at Kirkaldy, in 1723; Robert Fergusson, the Scottish poet, born at Edinburgh in 1750; and Dugald Stewart, born at Edinburgh in 1753. If, for a similar purpose, we come down to the last quarter of the century, five names at least will be sure to occur to us, in addition to that of Brougham— Thomas Campbell, born in Glasgow in 1777; Thomas Chalmers, born at Anstruther in Fifeshire in 1780; John Wilson, born at Paisley in 1785; Sir William Hamilton, born at Glasgow in 1788; Edward Irving, born at Annan in Dumfriesshire in 1792; and Thomas Carlyle, born near Ecclefechan, in the same county, in 1795. In this list we omit the distinguished contemporary Scottish names in physical science. We ought not, however, to omit the names of Sir James Mackintosh, born near Inverness in 1765, and James Mill, born at Montrose in 1773. The short life of Burns, if we choose him as the central figure of the group, connects all the persons named. The oldest of them was in the prime of life when Burns was born, and the youngest of them had seen the light before Burns died.

G

On glancing along this series of eminent Scotchmen
born in the eighteenth century, it will be seen that
they may be roughly distributed into two nearly equal
classes—men of philosophic intellect, devoted to the
work of general speculation, or thought as such; and
men of literary or poetic genius, whose works belong
more properly to the category of pure literary or artistic
effort.   In the one class may be ranked Reid, Hume,
Adam   Smith,   Dugald Stewart,   Mackintosh,   Mill,
Chalmers,   and   Sir William Hamilton ;   in the other,
Thomson,   Smollett, Robertson,   Fergusson,   Burns,
Scott, Jeffrey, Campbell, Wilson, Irving, and Carlyle.
Do not let us be mistaken. In using the phrases "philosophic intellect " and " literary genius " to denote the
distinction referred to, we do not imply anything of
accurate discrimination between the phrases themselves.
For aught that we care, the phrases may be reversed,
and the men of the one class may be styled men of
philosophic genius, and those of the other men of
literary habit and intellect.   If we prefer to follow the
popular usage in our application of the terms, it is not
with any intention of making out for the one class, by
the appropriation to it of the peculiar term " genius,"
a certificate of a higher kind of excellence than belongs
to the other.   Even according to the popular accepta-
tion of the term, several of those whom we have
included in the literary category—as, for **example,**

Robertson—must be denied the title of men of genius :
while, by no endurable definition of the term, could
the title of men of genius be refused to such men as
Adam Smith, Chalmers, and Hamilton. Nor even when
thus explained will our classification bear a very rigid
scrutiny. By a considerable portion of what may be
called the fundamental or unapparent half of his genius
Carlyle belongs to the class of speculative thinkers;
while, on the other hand, the case of Chalmers is one
in which the thinking or speculative faculty, which certainly belonged to him, was surcharged and deluged by
such a constant flood from the feelings that, instead
of ranking him with the thinkers as above, we might,
with equal or greater propriety, transpose him to
the other side, or even name him on both sides. His
thinking faculty, which was what he himself set most
store by, was so beset and begirt by his other and more
active dispositions that, instead of working on and on
through any resisting medium with iron continuity, it
discharged itself almost invariably, as soon as it touched
a subject, in large proximate generalizations.

On the whole, then, instead of the foregoing classification of eminent Scotchmen into men of speculation
and men of general literature, one might adopt as
equally serviceable a less formal classification which
the common satirical talk respecting Scotchmen will
suggest. The hard, cool, logical Scotchman : such is

the stereotyped phrase in which Englishmen describe the natives of North Britain. There is a sufficient amount of true perception in the phrase to justify its use; but the appreciation it involves reaches only to the surface. The well-known phrase, *perfervidum ingenium Scotorum*, used, Buchanan tells us, centuries ago on the Continent to express the idea of the Scottish character then universally current, and founded on a large induction of instances, is, in reality, far nearer to the fact. Without maintaining at present that *all* Scotchmen are perfervid,—that Scotchmen in general are, as we have seen it ingeniously argued, not cool, calculating, and cautious, but positively rash, fanatical, and tempestuous,—it will be enough to refer to the instances which prove at least that *some* Scotchmen have this character. The thing may be expressed thus :—On referring to the actual list of Scotchmen who have attained eminence by their writings or speeches in this or the last century, two types may be distinguished, in one or the other of which the Scottish mind seems necessarily to cast itself—(1) an intellectual type specifically Scottish, but Scottish only in the sense that it is the type which cultured Scottish minds assume when they devote themselves to the work of specific investigation ; and (2) a more popular type, characterizing those Scotchmen who, instead of pursuing the work of specific investigation, follow a career calling forth all the resources of thought and sentiment. Scotchmen of the first, or more fixed and formal, type are Reid, Smith, Hume, Mill, Mackintosh, and Hamilton ; in all of whom, notwithstanding their differences, we see that tendency towards metaphysical speculation for which the Scottish mind has become celebrated. Scotchmen of the other or popular type, partaking of the metaphysical tendency or not, but drawing their essential inspiration from the sentimental depths of the national character, are · Burns, Scott, Chalmers, Irving, and Carlyle. However we may choose to express it, the fact of this twofold forthgoing of the Scottish mind, either in the scholastic and logical direction marked out by one series of eminent predecessors, or in the popular and literary direction marked out by another series of eminent predecessors, cannot be denied.

After all, however, there *is,* classify and distinguish as we may, a remarkable degree of homogeneousness among Scotchmen. The people of North Britain are more homogeneous, have decidedly a more visible basis of common character, than the people of South Britain. A Scotchman may indeed be almost anything that is possible in this world. He may be a saint or a debauchee, a Christian or a sceptic, a spendthrift or a usurer, a soldier or a statesman, a poet or a statistician, a fool or a man of genius, clear-headed or confused-

headed, a Thomas Chalmers or a Joseph Hume, a dry
man of mere secular facts, or a man through whose
mind there roll for ever the stars and all mysteries.
Still, under every possible form of mental combination or activity, there will be found in every Scotchman something distinguishable as his birth-quality or
Scotticism.

What is this *Scotticism* of Scotchmen ?   What is this
ineradicable, universally-combinable element or peculiarity, breathed into the Scottish soul by those conditions of nature and of life which inhere in or hover over
the area of the Scottish earth, and which are repeated
in the same precise *ensemble* nowhere else ?   Comes it
from the hills, or the moors, or the mists, or any of
those other features of scenery and climate which distinguish bleak and rugged Scotland from green and
fertile England ?   In part, doubtless, from these, as
from all else that is Scottish.   But there are hills, and
moors, and mists where Scotchmen are not bred ; and
it is rather in the long series of the memorable things
that have been done on the Scottish hills and moors—
the acts which the retrospective eye sees flashing
through the old Scottish mists—that one is to seek
the origin and explanation of whatever Scotticism is.
Now, as compared with England at least, that which
has come down to the natives of Scotland as something peculiar, generated by the series of past trans-

actions of which their country has been the scene, is an intense spirit of nationality.

No nation in the world is more factitious than the Scotch, none more composite. If in England there have been Celts, Romans, Saxons, Danes, and Normans, in Scotland there have been Celts, Romans, Norwegians, Danes, Anglo-Saxons, and Anglo-Normans. The only difference of any consequence in this respect probably is that, whereas in England the Celtic element is derived chiefly from the British or Welsh, and the Gothic element chiefly from the Teutonic or Continental-German source, in Scotland the Gaels have furnished most of the Celtic, and the Scandinavian Germans most of the Gothic element. Nor, if we regard the agencies that have acted intellectually on the two nations, shall we find Scotland to have been less notably affected from without than England. To mention only one circumstance, the Reformation in Scotland was marked by a much more decided importation of new modes of thinking and new social forms than the Reformation in the sister country. But, though quite as factitious as the English nation, the Scottish, by reason of its very smallness, has always possessed a more intense consciousness of its nationality, and a greater liability to be acted upon throughout its whole substance by a common thought or a common feeling. Even as late as the year 1707 the entire population of Scotland did not exceed one million of individuals; and if, going farther back, we fancy this small nation placed on the frontier of one so much larger, and obliged continually to defend itself against the attacks of so powerful a neighbour, we can have no difficulty in conceiving how, in the smaller nation, the feeling of a central life would be sooner developed and kept more continuously active. The sentiment of nationality is essentially negative. It is the sentiment of a people which has been taught to recognise its own individuality by incessantly marking the line of exclusion between itself and others. Almost all the great movements of Scotland, as a nation, have accordingly been of a negative character. They have been movements of self-defence. The War of National Independence against the Edwards, the Non-Episcopal struggle in the reigns of the Charleses, the Non-Intrusion controversy of later times, may be taken as examples. The very motto of Scotland is negative: *Nemo me impune lacesset.* It is different with England. There have of course been negative movements in England too, but these have been movements of one faction or part of the English people against another; and the activity of the English nation, as a whole, has consisted, not in preserving its own individuality from external attack, but in fully and genially evolving the various elements which it finds within itself, or in powerful positive exertions of its strength upon what lies outside of it.

The first and most natural form of what we have called the Scotticism of Scotchmen—that is, of the peculiarity which differences them from people of other countries, and more expressly from Englishmen—is this *amor patriæ*, this inordinate intensity of national feeling. There are very few Scotchmen who, whatever they may pretend, are devoid of this pride in being Scotchmen. Penetrate to the heart of any Scotchman, even the most Anglified or the most philosophic that can be found, and there will certainly be seen a remnant in it of loving regard for the little land that lies north of the Tweed. And what eminent Scotchman can be named in whose constitution a larger or smaller proportion of the *amor Scotiæ* has not been visible? In some of the foremost such men, as in Burns, Scott, and Wilson, this *amor Scotiæ* has been present as even a professed ingredient of their genius, a sentiment determining, to a great extent, the style and matter of all that they have written or attempted:—

> " The rough bur-thistle spreading wide
>   Amang the bearded bear,
> I turned the weeder-clips aside,
>   And spared the symbol dear.
>   No nation, no station
>   My envy e'er could raise ;
>   A Scot still, but blot still,
>   I knew nae higher praise."

In reading the writings of such men, one is perpetually reminded, in the most direct manner, that these writings are to be regarded as belonging to a strictly national literature. But even in those Scotchmen in the determination of whose intellectual efforts the *amor Scotiæ* has acted no such ostensible part the presence of some mental reference to, or intermittent communication of sentiment with, the land of their birth is almost sure to be detected. The speculations of Reid, Hume, and Adam Smith, and, in some degree, also, those of Chalmers, were on matters interesting not to Scotchmen alone, but to the human race as such; and yet, precisely as these men enunciated their generalities intended for the whole world in good broad Scotch, so had they all, after their different ways, a genuine Scottish relish for Scottish humours, jokes, and antiquities. The same thing is true of Carlyle, a power as he is recognised to be not in Scottish only, but in all European literature. Even James Mill, who, more than most Scotchmen, succeeded in conforming, both in speech and in writing, to English habits and requirements, relapsed into the Scot when he listened to a Scottish song or told a Scottish anecdote. But perhaps the most interesting example of the appearance of an intense *amor Scotiæ* where, from the nature of the case, it could have been least expected, is afforded by the writings of Sir William Hamilton. If there is a man now alive conspicuous among his contemporaries for the exercise on the most magnificent scale of an intellect the most pure and abstract, that man is Sir William;[1] and yet, not even when discussing the philosophy of the unconditioned or perfecting the theory of syllogism, does he forget his Scottish lineage. With what glee, in his notes, or in stray passages in his dissertations themselves, does he seize every opportunity of adding to the proofs that speculation in general has been largely affected by the stream of specific Scottish thought—quoting, for example, the saying of Scaliger, " *Les Ecossois sont bons Philosophes ;*" or dwelling on the fact that at one time almost every continental university had a Scottish professorship of philosophy, specially so named ; or reviving the memories of defunct Balfours, and Duncans, and Chalmerses, and Dalgarnos, and other " *Scoti extra Scotiam agentes* " of other centuries ; or startling his readers with such genealogical facts as that Immanuel Kant and Sir Isaac Newton had Scottish grandfathers, and that the celebrated French metaphysician Destutt Tracy was, in reality, but a transmogrified Scotchman of the name of Stott ! We know few things more refreshing than such evidences of strong national feeling in such a man. It is the Scottish Stagirite not ashamed of the

---

[1] Sir William died in 1856, four years after this was written.

bonnet and plaid; it is the philosopher in whose veins flows the blood of a Covenanter.

Even now, when Scotchmen, their native country having been so long merged in the higher unity of Great Britain, labour altogether in the service of this higher unity, and forget or set aside the smaller, they are still liable to be affected characteristically in all that they do by the consciousness that they are Scotchmen. This will be found true whether we regard those Scotchmen who work side by side with Englishmen in the conduct of British public affairs or British commerce, or those Scotchmen who vie with Englishmen in the walks of British authorship and literature. In either case the Scotchman is distinguished from the Englishman by this, that he carries the consciousness of his nationality about with him. Were he, indeed, disposed to forget it, the banter on the subject to which he is perpetually exposed in the society of his English friends and acquaintances would serve to keep him in mind of it. It is the same now with the individual Scotchman cast among Englishmen as it was with the Scottish nation when it had to defend its frontier against the English armies. He is in the position of a smaller body placed in contact with a larger one, and rendered more conscious of his individuality by the constant necessity of asserting it. But this self-assertion of a Scotchman among Englishmen, this constant feeling "I am a

Scotchman," rests, like the feeling of nationality itself, on a prior assertion of what is in fact a negative. For a Scotchman to be always thinking "I am a Scotchman" is, in the circumstances now under view, tantamount to always thinking "I am *not* an Englishman." The Englishman, on the other hand, has no corresponding feeling. As a member of the larger body, whose corporate activity has always been positive rather than negative, the Englishman simply acts out harmoniously his English instincts and tendencies, the feeling of not being a Scotchman never (except in the case of a stray Englishman located in Scotland) either spontaneously remaining in his mind or being roused in it by banter. The Scotchman who works in the general field of British activity has his thoughts conditioned, to some extent at least, by the negative of not being an Englishman ; the Englishman thinks under no such limitation.

This leads us to a more intimate definition of the peculiarity of Scottish as compared with English thought. The rudest and most natural form of what we have called the Scotticism of Scotchmen consists, we have hitherto been saying, in simple consciousness of nationality, simple *amor Scotiæ*, or, in more restricted circumstances, the simple feeling of not being an Englishman. There are some Scotchmen, however, in whom this first and most natural form of Scotticism is

not very well pronounced, and who are either emancipated from it, or think that they are. We know not a
few Scots who have really succeeded in transferring
their enthusiastic regards from Scotland to the higher
unity of Great Britain—men who, sometimes speaking
in their own Scottish accent, sometimes in an accent
almost purely English, find the objects of their solicitude and admiration, not in the land lying north of
the Tweed, but rather in England, with her rich green
parks and fields, her broad ecclesiastical hierarchy, her
noble halls of learning, her majestic and varied literature, the full and generous character of her manly
people. We know Scotchmen whose sentiment is more
deeply stirred by Shakespeare's famous apostrophe to
" this England " than by Scott's to the land of brown
heath and shaggy wood. And, as Scotland and England are now united, such men are becoming more
numerous. But even they shall not escape. If their
native quality of Scotticism does not survive in them
in the more palpable and open form of mere national
feeling, mere *amor Scotiæ*, it survives, nevertheless, in
an intellectual habit, having the same root, and as
indestructible. And what is this habit ? The popular
charges of dogmatism, opinionativeness, pugnacity, and
the like, brought against Scotchmen by Englishmen,
are so many approximations to a definition of it. For
our part, we should say that the special habit or

peculiarity which distinguishes the intellectual manifestations of Scotchmen—that, in short, in which the
Scotticism of Scotchmen most intimately consists—is
the habit of *emphasis*. All Scotchmen are *emphatic*.
If a Scotchman is a fool, he gives such emphasis to the
nonsense he utters as to be considerably more insufferable
than a fool of any other country; if a Scotchman is a
man of genius, he gives such emphasis to the good
things he has to communicate that they have a su-
premely good chance of being at once or very soon
attended to. This habit of emphasis is exactly that
perfervidum ingenium Scotorum which used to be remarked some centuries ago wherever Scotchmen were
known. But emphasis is perhaps a better word than
fervour. Many Scotchmen are fervid too, but not all;
but all, absolutely all, are emphatic. No one will call
Joseph Hume a fervid man, but he is certainly emphatic. And so with David Hume, or Reid, or Adam
Smith, or any of those colder-natured Scotchmen of
whom we have spoken. Fervour cannot be predicated
of them, but they had plenty of emphasis. In men like
Burns, or Chalmers, or Irving, on the other hand, there
was both emphasis and fervour; so also with Carlyle;
and so, in a still more curious combination, with Sir
William Hamilton. And, as we distinguish emphasis
from fervour, so would we distinguish it from per-
severance. Scotchmen are said to be persevering, but

the saying is not universally true. Scotchmen are or
are not morally persevering, but all Scotchmen are intellectually emphatic. Emphasis, we repeat, intellectual
emphasis, the habit of laying stress on certain things
rather than co-ordinating all : in this consists what is
essential in the Scotticism of Scotchmen. And, as this
observation is empirically verified by the very manner
in which Scotchmen enunciate their words in ordinary
talk, so it might be deduced scientifically from what
has been said regarding the nature and effects of the
feeling of nationality. The habit of thinking emphatically is a necessary result of thinking much in the
presence of, and in resistance to, a negative ; it is the
habit of a people that has been accustomed to act on
the defensive, rather than of a people peacefully self-
evolved and accustomed to act positively; it is the
habit of Protestantism rather than of Catholicism, of
Presbyterianism rather than of Episcopacy, of Dissent
rather than of Conformity.

The greatest effects which the Scottish mind has yet
produced on the world (and these effects, by the confession of Englishmen themselves, have not been small)
have been the results, in part at least, of this national
habit of emphasis. Until towards the close of last
century, the special department of labour in which
Scotchmen had, to any great extent, exerted themselves
so as to make a figure in the general intellectual world,

was the department of Philosophy, metaphysical and
dialectic. Their triumphs in this department are historical. What is called the Scottish Philosophy constitutes, in the eyes of all who know anything of
history, a most important stage in the intellectual
evolution of modern Europe. From the time of those
old Duncans, Balfours, and Dalgarnos, mentioned by
Sir William Hamilton, who discoursed on philosophy,
and wrote dialectical treatises in Latin in all the cities
of the Continent, down to our own days, one can point
to a succession of Scottish thinkers in whom the interest
in metaphysical studies was kept alive, and by whose
labours new contributions to mental science were continually made. It was by the Scottish mind, in fact,
that the modern philosophy was conducted to that
point where Kant and the Germans took it up. The
qualifications of the Scottish mind for this task were,
doubtless, various. Perhaps there was something in
that special combination of the Celtic and the Scandinavian out of which the Scottish nation, for the most
part, took its rise, to produce an aptitude for dialectical
exercises. Farther, it would not be altogether fanciful
to suppose that those very national struggles of the
Scotch in the course of which they acquired so strong a
sense of their national individuality—that is, of the
distinction between all that was Scotch and all that
was not Scotch—served, in a rough way, to facilitate

H

for all Scotchmen that fundamental idea of the distinction between the *Ego* and the *Non-Ego* the clear and rigorous apprehension of which is the first step in philosophy and the one test of the philosopher. In a still more important respect, however, one might trace the success of the Scottish mind in philosophy to the national habit of intellectual emphasis. A Scotchman, when he thinks, cannot so easily and comfortably as the Englishman repose on an upper level of propositions co-ordinated for him by tradition, sweet feeling, and pleasant circumstance. That necessity of his nature which leads him to emphasise certain things, rather than to take all things together in their established co-ordination, drives him down and still down in search of certain generalities whereon he may see that all can be built. It was this habit of emphasis, this inability to rest on the level of sweetly-composed experience, that led Hume to scepticism; it was the same habit, the same inability, conjoined with more of faith and reverence, that led Reid to lay down in the chasm of Hume's scepticism certain blocks of ultimate propositions or principles, capable of being individually enumerated, and yet, as he thought, forming a sufficient basement for all that men think or believe. And the same tendency is visible among Scotchmen now. It amazes Scotchmen at the present day to see on what proximate propositions even Englishmen who are celebrated as thinkers can rest their speculations. The truth is that, if Scotchmen have, so far, a source of superiority over Englishmen in their habit of dwelling only on the emphatic, they have also in this same habit a source of inferiority. Quietism, mysticism, that soft, meditative disposition which takes things for granted in the co-ordination established by mere life and usage, pouring into the confusion thus externally given the oil of an abounding inner joy, interpenetrating all and harmonizing all—these are, for the most part, alien to the Scotchman. His walk is not by the meadows, the wheat fields, the green lanes, and the ivy-clad parish churches, where all is gentle, and antique, and fertile, but by the bleak sea-shore which parts the certain from the limitless, where there is doubt in the seamew's shriek, and where it is well if in the advancing tide he can find footing on a rock among the tangle. But this very tendency of his towards what is intellectually extreme injures his sense of proportion in what is concrete and actual; and hence it is that, when he leaves the field of abstract thought, and betakes himself to creative literature, he so seldom produces anything comparable, in fulness, wealth, and harmoniousness, to the imaginations of a Chaucer or a Shakespeare. The highest genius, indeed, involves also the capability of the intellectually extreme, and, accordingly, in the writings of those great Englishmen, just as

in those of the living English poet Tennyson, there are
strokes in abundance of that pure intellectual emphasis
in which the Scotchman delights ; but then there is
also with them such a genial acceptance of all things,
great or small, in their established co-ordination that
the flashes of emphasis are as if they came not from a
battle done on an open moor, but from a battle transacting itself in the depths of a forest.   Among Scottish
thinkers, Mackintosh is the one that approaches nearest
to the English model ; and this may be accounted for
by the fact that much of what he did consisted, from
the necessities of the object-matter of his speculations,
in judicious compromise.

But even in the field of literature we need not abandon
the Scotchman. His habit of emphasis has here enabled
him to do good service too. His entry on this field,
however, was later than his entry on the field of philosophy. True, there had been, contemporary with the
Scottish philosophers, or even anterior to them, Scottish
poets and general prose-writers of note— Dunbar,
Gawain Douglas, King James I., of Scotland, Buchanan, Sir David Lindsay, Henryson, Drummond,
Allan Ramsay, and the like. True, also, in those
snatches of popular ballad and song which came down
from generation to generation in Scotland—many of
them written by no one knows whom, and almost all
of them overflowing with either humour or melancholy

—there was at once a fountain and a promise of an exquisite national literature. One can think of old Nicol Burn, the "violer," out on his rounds in the Yarrow district, and singing as he played :—

> " But Minstrel Burn cannot assuage
>   His woes while time endureth,
>   To see the changes of this age
>   Which fleeting time procureth.
>   Full many a place stands in hard case
>   Where joy was wont beforrow,
>   With Humes that dwelt on Leader braes,
>   And Scotts that dwelt on Yarrow."

There was literature in the times when such old strains were sung. But the true avatar of the Scottish mind in modern literature came later than the manifestation of the same mind in philosophy. Were we to fix a precise date for it, we should name the period of Burns's first visit to Edinburgh and familiar meetings with the men of literary talent and distinction then assembled there.

Edinburgh was, indeed, even then a literary capital, boasting of its Monboddos, Stewarts, Robertsons, Blairs, Mackenzies, and Gregorys, men who had already begun the race of literary rivalry with their contemporaries south of the Tweed. But, so far as the literary excellence of these men did not depend on their participation in that tendency to abstract thinking

which had already produced its special fruit in the
Scottish Philosophy, it consisted in little more than a
reflection or imitation of what was already common and
acknowledged in the prior or contemporary literature
of South Britain.   To write essays such as those of the
Spectator ; to be master of a style which Englishmen
should pronounce pure, and to produce compositions in
that style worthy of being ranked with the compositions
of English authors : such was the aim and aspiration of
Edinburgh *literati* between whom and their London
cousins there was all the difference that there is
between the latitude of Edinburgh and the latitude of
London, between the daily use of the broad Scotch
dialect and the daily use of the classic English.
For Scotland this mere imitation of English models
was a poor and unsatisfactory vein of literary enterprise.
What was necessary was the appearance of some man
of genius who should flash through all that, and who,
by the application to literature, or the art of universal
expression, of that same Scottish habit of emphasis
which had already produced such striking and original
results in philosophy, should teach the Scottish nation
its true power in literature, and show a first example of
it.   Such a man was Burns.   He it was who, uniting
emotional fervour with intellectual emphasis, and drawing his inspiration from all those depths of sentiment
in the Scottish people which his predecessors, the

philosophers, had hardly so much as touched, struck for the first time a new chord, and revealed for the first time what a Scottish writer could do by trusting. to the whole wealth of Scottish resources. From the time of Burns, accordingly, there has been a series of eminent literary Scotchmen quite different from that series of hard logical Scotchmen who had till then been the most conspicuous representatives of their country in the eyes of the reading public of Great Britain—a series of Scotchmen displaying the power of emphatic sentiment and emphatic expression as strikingly as their predecessors had displayed the power of emphatic reasoning. While, the old philosophic energy of Scotland still remained unexhausted—the honours of Reid, Hume, Smith, and Stewart passing on to such men as Brown, Mill, Mackintosh, and Hamilton (in favour of the last of whom even Germany has paused in her philosophic interregnum)—the special literary energy which had been awakened in the country descended along another line in the persons of Scott, Jeffrey, Chalmers, Campbell, Wilson, and Carlyle. Considering the amount of influence exerted by such men upon the whole spirit and substance of British literature, considering how large a share of the whole literary produce of Great Britain in the nineteenth century has come either from them or from other Scotchmen, and considering what a stamp of peculiarity marks all that portion of this produce which *is* of Scottish origin, are we not entitled to say that the rise and growth of recent Scottish literature is as notable a historical phenomenon as the rise and growth of the Scottish philosophy? Considering, moreover, how lately Scotland has entered on this literary field, how little time she has had to display her powers, how recently she was in this respect savage, and how much of her savage vitality yet remains to be articulated in civilized books, may we not hope that her literary avatar is but beginning and has a goodly course yet to run? From Solway to Caithness we hear a loud *Amen.*

III.

THE LIFE AND POETRY OF SHELLEY.

III.

THE LIFE AND POETRY OF SHELLEY.[1]

CELEBRATED for many a transaction belonging to the history of Italy, the fifty miles of Italian coast which lie between Leghorn in Tuscany and Spezzia in the Sardinian states possess also, in virtue of certain events of which they were the scene in the summer of 1822, a peculiar interest in connexion with British poetry.

Byron and Shelley were then both living there. Voluntary exiles, for similar reasons, from their native land, and already personally known to each other, they had been residing separately for several years in different parts of Italy; during the few immediately preceding months they had been living in the same town of Pisa, seeing each other daily, and becoming better acquainted with each other; and now again they had

[1] *Macmillan's Magazine*, September 1860.

just parted—Byron to take up his summer-quarters at
Leghorn, and Shelley his at a lonely spot near Lerici,
in the Gulf of Spezzia. The two poets were thus, for
the time, separated by the whole distance of the fifty
intervening miles. A circumstance which made their
separation rather unfortunate at the moment was that
a third English poet—Mr. Leigh Hunt—was then on
his way to Italy to join them. While Byron and
Shelley were still together at Pisa, it had been arranged
that Mr. Hunt should come out to them, and that the
three should start a political and literary periodical
which Byron had projected, and which, published at
Pisa, should electrify Europe. Now that Byron and
Shelley had separated, the arrangement had to be
modified. Mr. Hunt was to join Lord Byron at
Leghorn; they were to be the active partners in the
periodical; and Shelley was but to visit them now
and then, and help them as much as he could from
his retreat at Lerici. Nor did the fifty miles of distance matter very much. Both Byron and Shelley
were passionately fond of the sea; and yachting in
that lovely bit of the Mediterranean was one of the
pleasures that made them prefer Italy to England.
Byron had just bought a beautiful craft, built like a
man-of-war brig, to lie in Leghorn harbour, and be
ready at a moment's notice to carry him and his
friends Roberts and Trelawny wherever they chose;

and Shelley, according to his more modest tastes and means, had procured a small open pleasure-boat, to lie on the beach under the hill which rose behind his solitary house, and to carry himself, Mrs. Shelley, and any friend that might chance to visit them, along the Bay of Spezzia, or even southward, at a stretch, as far as Leghorn. With such means of communication, there was little fear but that Byron, Hunt, and Shelley would be often together! Byron's dangerous-looking craft, the *Bolivar*, showing her brazen teeth through her miniature port-holes, would often be cruising north-wards in the direction of Spezzia, and Shelley's white-sailed boat would be seen coyly tacking to meet her; and, in the course of a month or two, the Italian pre-ventive-men along the shore would know both well as the vessels of the English poet-lord and his mysterious fellow-countryman! Alas! and, to this day [1860], if we consider only what was historically possible, those two vessels or their successors might still have been cruising familiarly, each with its owner aboard, on the same tract of sea! Leigh Hunt, the oldest of the three poets, was alive among us but a few months ago, at the age of seventy-five; had Byron lived, he would now have been seventy-two; Shelley, had he lived, would have been sixty-eight. In the summer of which we speak Leigh Hunt was in his thirty-ninth year, Byron in his thirty-fifth, Shelley in his thirtieth.

Looking at Shelley, as we can fancy him standing on
the beach at Lerici, what do we see? A man still
young, rather tall, but bent a little at the shoulders
from weakness—with a very small head, and hair
naturally dark-brown and curling, but now prematurely
tinged with grey ; the face also singularly small, with a
pale or pinkish-pale complexion, large spiritual-looking
eyes, very delicate features, and an expression altogether
graceful, etherial, and feminine. Could we hear him
speak, the impression would be completed by his voice.
This is described as having been very high and shrill, so
that some one who heard it unexpectedly in a mixed
company compared it to the scream of a peacock. On
the whole, seen or heard even for the first time, he was
a man to excite a feeling of interest, and a curiosity as
to his previous history.

Born the heir to an English baronetcy, and to more
than the usual wealth and consideration attending that
rank, the whole life of Shelley had been a war against
custom. At Eton the sensitive boy, almost girlish in
his look and demeanour, had nerved himself, with meek
obstinacy, though with secret tears, against every part
of the established system—not only against the tyranny
of his fellows, but also against the teaching of the
masters. It had been the same when he went to
Oxford. He was then a Greek scholar, a writer of
verses, an insatiable student of the metaphysics of

Berkeley and Hume, an incessant reasoner with any one that would reason with him on points of philosophy or politics, and in every such argument an avowed Revolutionist, and at least a hypothetical Atheist. In the rooms of his college, or along the streets, his shrill voice might be heard attacking Christianity, Religion, the very idea of a God. He was frantically earnest on this subject, as if, by compelling discussion of it, he were digging at the root of all evil. At length, tired of merely talking with his acquaintances, he sent a printed statement of his opinions to the University authorities, challenging them to an argument with him as to the necessity or utility of any religious belief. The act was ghastly, and the reply of the authorities was his instant expulsion from the University. His family were shocked, and could not tell what to make of such a youth ; and, at the age of seventeen, he re- moved to London to live as his own master. There he printed and privately distributed a number of copies of his *Queen Mab*, expanding and illustrating the poetical Atheism of the text in appended prose notes. He introduced himself by letter to men and women of genius, trying to enlist them in the great war which he had begun, and into which he thought the whole intel- lectual world must follow, against Statecraft and Priest- craft. He read with avidity Godwin's "Political Justice" —in the doctrines of which book he found a new social

gospel; and he resolved from that hour to square all
his actions by what he considered strict justice, without
reference to the opinions of others. At this time he
had, by arrangement with his family, about 200*l.* a
year; which income he was able to increase, by borrow-
ing on his expectations, or in other ways. His own
manner of living was extremely temperate ; indeed, for
several years he was a vegetarian in diet and drank only
water. He had thus money to spend on objects that
moved his charity. He was continually in quest of
such objects. Every social anomaly, almost every social
inequality, affected him intensely. If he saw a shivering beggar in the street asking alms beside a carriage,
his longing was nothing less than to add the beggar and
the carriage together on the spot and divide the sum by
two. The sole use of his own money seemed to him to
be to mitigate, as far as he could, these social inequalities.
He did the most extraordinary and the most generous
things. To give away twenty or thirty pounds, where
he fancied it would relieve distress, was nothing to him.
He involved himself in debt and serious inconvenience
by repetitions of such acts of benevolence. Nor was it
only with money that he was generous. His society,
his sympathy, beyond the range of the intellectual
occupations in which he delighted, were given, by preference, to the outcast and the wretched. It was in the
same spirit of contempt for usage that, when, in his

twentieth year, his affections were engaged, he
married the object of them—the daughter of a retired
tradesman. After three years of married life, spent in
different places, and latterly not happily, he and his
wife had separated by mutual consent, she returning
with her two children to her father's house. Shelley
then formed the new connexion which ended in his
second marriage, and went abroad to travel. On his
return he resided for eighteen months in London—his
fortune increased about this time, by his grandfather's
death, to 1,000*l.* a year; which continued to be his
income as long as he lived. This was the time too of
his becoming acquainted with Leigh Hunt, and, through
him, with Keats. One of his first acts on becoming
acquainted with Leigh Hunt was to offer him 100*l.*;
and Mr. Hunt himself has recorded that this was but
the beginning of a series of kindnesses almost unprece-
dented in the annals of friendship. On one occasion
of exigency he gave Hunt 1,400*l.* It was while Shelley
was residing in London in 1815 that *Alastor, or The
Spirit of Solitude* was composed. Early in 1816 he
and his companion again went abroad. They resided
for about a year and a half in Switzerland and
in Italy. It was in Switzerland that they had
first become acquainted with Lord Byron, who was
then living there. On their return to England they
went to Bath ; and here it was that Shelley received the

terrible news of the suicide of his wife. To the horror
of the event itself was added the public scandal which
followed when the relatives of the unhappy woman
instituted a suit in Chancery to prevent Shelley from
taking back his children. They grounded their suit on
the fact that Shelley was an avowed Atheist. On this,
as in itself a sufficiently legal plea, Lord Chancellor
Eldon gave judgment in their favour. As far as the
newspapers could carry the report of the trial, the
name and the antecedents of "the Atheist Shelley" had
thus been blazoned over Britain. When the judgment
was given, Shelley was residing with his second wife—
Mary Wollstonecraft Godwin—at Great Marlow in
Buckinghamshire. Here he had organised a regular
system of charity. He had pensioners among the
agricultural labourers and the poor silk-weavers all
round; he even studied medicine, and walked the
hospitals in London, that he might be of use to the
sick. But neither in Great Marlow, nor anywhere else
in England, could the philanthropy of a man who bore
the brand of Atheist be trusted or tolerated. His very
pensioners shrank from him, and took his money sus-
piciously. Strongly sensitive to such distrust, and
fearing also future interferences of the law of England
with his liberty, he had resolved, if even at the sacrifice
of all his rights of inheritance to the family property,
to leave England for ever. In the spring of 1818 he

had carried out the resolution by going to Italy. Before
leaving England, he had written his *Revolt of Islam*,
and many other pieces of verse and prose which now
appear in his collected works ; but the four years that
had elapsed since his arrival in Italy had been the
period of what are now esteemed his finest productions.
During those four years—residing at Venice, at Rome,
at Naples, at Florence, and finally, as we have seen, at
Pisa—he had written his *Prometheus Unbound,* his
Cenci, his *Hellas,* his *Julian and Maddalo,* his *Epi-
psychidion,* his *Witch of Atlas,* his *Ode to Naples,* and his
Adonais, besides his translations in prose and verse
from Plato, Calderon, the Homeric poets, and Goethe.
During the same period, also, he had begun to take a
more direct interest than before in the current politics
of Britain and of Europe—working down his general
doctrines respecting Man and Society into strong
Radical lyrics, and satires on the Liverpool and Castle-
reagh administration, calculated to do rough service at
home; and throwing much of his energy simultaneously
into what we now call the cause of the oppressed
nationalities. He had, indeed, a passion for being
practical, and had recently spent a great deal of
money on an attempt, which did not succeed, to
establish a steamboat between Leghorn and Mar-
seilles.

Such, from his birth, had been the twenty-nine years

of wandering, of wild clamour and agony, of fitful
ecstasy of mind and heart, that had brought the poet,
a kind of intellectual outcast, to his Salvator-Rosa
solitude under the pine-hills of Spezzia, sloping to
the sea.   Part of all this past life of error and suffering (for time is merciful) had, doubtless, been left
behind, melted and softened in the thin air of recollection ; but part remained incorporate in the very
being of the sufferer, not to be dissolved away even
by the Italian sun, or soothed by the softness of the
bluest heaven.

What proportion of the past had faded, and what remained, it might be difficult to say.   Among the things
that had faded, one might say with some certainty, was
the early crudity of his exulting Atheism.

Even at first, had not Shelley himself assumed the
name of Atheist, and employed it as a signature, and
shrieked it wherever he went, and seemed sometimes to
riot in the very horror it produced, it may be doubted
whether, from any study of his poems, the name would
ever have been attached to him.   He would have been
named, much more probably, a Pantheist, a Platonist,
or the like.   A recognition of the supernatural, of at
least a spirit of intellectual beauty as pervading all
visible things, of human life as but an evanescent incar-
nation and short local battle of principles that have their
origin behind time and beyond the stars, seems the one

characteristic of Shelley's poetry from the first, which
if we do not attend to, it has no logical coherence. In
all our literature it would be difficult to find a soul that
was less the soul of a Secularist. Only remember, in
contrast with him, Bunyan's typical Atheist in the
"Pilgrim's Progress." Christian and Hopeful are there
toiling along on their road across a great plain, when
they perceive afar off one coming softly and all alone
meeting them, with his back towards that part of the
horizon behind which was the Zion to which they were
bound. This is "Atheist," who, when he comes up to
them, announces to them, with a leering positiveness,
that it is all a mistake—that there is no God and no
Zion, and that they may as well go back with him, and
snap their thumbs at being rid once for all of that
troublesome delusion. Not so, certainly, at any time
with Shelley ! If he denies Zion and Christianity, and
assails Christian and Hopeful for believing in them, it
is as one walking, with mad eagerness, while he does
so, in the same direction with them, scanning as intently
the distant sky, and blaspheming sideways in their ears
what he does not see, not because his eyes have ceased
one moment to look for it, but out of a wild sorrow
that it is not to be seen. A gleam, and one fancies he
would falter in the middle of his talk, he would start
and shade his eyes to gaze, he would fall to the ground
weeping ! Now, although there is no evidence that the

gleam ever came, though he still in his later years, as in his earlier, kept talking sideways at Christian and Hopeful in language which made them shudder, yet not only did he not cease to hurry on with them, but the very language of his sarcasm underwent a modification. Mr. Browning has stated it as his belief that, had Shelley lived, he would have ranged himself finally with the Christians. I do not feel that we are entitled to say so much as this ; for his latest letters show, I think, that much of what had been accounted, in this respect, the darkest peculiarity of his life, still remained with him.

Of what else remained that which was perhaps most obvious to those about him was the shattered state of his nerves. Always of weak health, nothing but his temperate habits could have kept him alive so long; and now he was often racked by a pulmonary pain, which seemed to augur that, in any case, he had not many years to live. But, beyond this, the morbid nervous excitement induced by such a life as his had been had begun to manifest itself in that abnormal action of the senses which makes men subject to visions, apparitions, and the terrors of waking dream. Various instances of such hallucinations, or nervous paroxysms, are recorded by his biographers. Thus, while he was staying at Great Marlow, he alarmed his friends and the neighbourhood by a story of a

with their new boat, resolved to set out in her to welcome Hunt. The weather had been overpoweringly hot, and the sea swollen and louring; but on the 1st of July a fine breeze sprang up, and they weighed for Leghorn. They performed the voyage in seven hours and a half, and anchored that night in Leghorn harbour beside the *Bolivar*, on board of which they slept. Next day, and for five days more, there were greetings of Hunt and his family, journeys with them and Byron to Pisa and other places, and much talk about the prospects of the new periodical. Unluckily, on account of some fray in Byron's house, which had brought an Italian servant of his within the grip of the Tuscan police, his Lordship had taken a sudden determination to leave Tuscany; and Shelley's chief care was to get such arrangements made as would prevent Hunt from being inconvenienced by this change of plan. He did all he could to secure this; and on the 8th of July, taking leave of Hunt, Byron, and others, he and Williams set out on their return to Lerici. An English sailor lad, named Charles Vivian, accompanied them in the boat. There were some fears for the weather, which for some days had been calm and sultry, but was now changed; but Shelley could not be persuaded to remain. The boat had not gone many miles, when one of the terrible squalls that occur in that part of the Mediterranean came on, and the friends left at Leghorn became anxious. Captain Roberts, who had been watching the boat on her homeward track with a glass from Leghorn lighthouse, saw her last, when the storm came on, off Via Reggio, at some distance from the shore, hugging the wind with a press of canvas. The storm then spread rapidly like a dark mist, and blotted out that part of the horizon, enveloping the distant little boat and several larger vessels that were also out. When the storm passed onwards from that quarter, Captain Roberts looked again, and saw every vessel except the little one, which had vanished. Within that storm had been the apparition of the naked babe!——For days and days there was great anxiety among the friends on shore. At length the sea itself told all that ever was to be known of the mystery, by washing ashore the three bodies—that of Shelley, that of Williams, and that of the boy Vivian —on different parts of the coast. The body of Shelley was burnt on a pyre of wood, heaped with wine, salt, frankincense, and perfumes, near the spot where it had been cast ashore, Byron, Hunt, Trelawny and others assisting at the ceremony. The collected ashes were conveyed to Rome and there buried.

Whatever rank one may be disposed to assign, all in all, to Shelley among English Poets, no reader can deny that his genius was of the poetical order, that he pos-

sessed in a singular degree the faculty of ideality, of
pure imagination. His larger poems are well and even
carefully conceived as wholes, according to the peculiar
kind of constructive art of which they are specimens.
The language is logically precise, easy, graceful, and
luxuriant; the versification is natural, various, and
musical; and there are individual passages of acute
and even comprehensive philosophical meaning, of
powerful and delicate description, of weirdly and exquisite phantasy, and of tender and concentrated feeling. In his descriptions and visual fancies one notices,
among other things, a wonderfully fine sense of colour.
Thus Asia, in the *Prometheus Unbound*, expecting, in a
vale of the Indian Caucasus, the arrival of her sister
Oceanid, Panthea :—

" This is the season, this the day, the hour ;
  At sunrise thou shouldst come, sweet sister mine.
  Too long denied, too long delaying, come !
  The point of one white star is quivering still,
  Deep in the orange light of widening morn
  Beyond the purple mountains. Through a chasm
  Of wind-divided mist the darker lake
  Reflects it : now it wanes : it gleams again
  As the waves fade, and as the burning threads
  Of woven cloud unravel in the thin air :
  'Tis lost ; and through yon peaks of cloud-like snow
  The roseate sunlight quivers : hear I not
  The Æolian music of her sea-green plumes
  Winnowing the crimson dawn ? "

Perhaps one of the finest continuous passages in all the larger poems is the concluding portion of the same drama, where, partly in choruses of unseen spirits, and partly in dialogue between Prometheus and the Oceanids in a forest near his cave, the glorious state of the emancipated world of the Promethean era, when Jove is dethroned, and Love and Justice reign, is set forth in mystic allegory. The following speech of Panthea may serve as a specimen of the part that is in dialogue. The new or Promethean earth is figured by the vision of a vast solid sphere, as of crystal, filled with multitudinous shapes and colours, yet all miraculously inter-transpicuous, which is seen rushing, as in a whirlwind of harmony, through an opening of the forest, grinding, as it wheels, a brook that flows beneath into an azure mist of light, and whirling grass, trees, and flowers into a kneaded mass of aerial emerald. Within this strange orb the Spirit of the Earth is seen asleep, like a wearied child, pillowed on its alabaster arms, which are laid over its folded wings. Its lips are seen moving as in a smiling dream ; and from a star upon its forehead there shoot swords and beams of fire, which whirl as the orb whirls, and transpierce its otherwise opaque bulk with radiant lightnings. In the light of these incessant shafts all the secrets of the earth's interior, from the circumference to the core, are revealed in continuous translucence :—

" Infinite mines of adamant and gold,
  Valueless glories, unimagined gems,
  And caverns on crystalline columns poised,
  With vegetable silver overspread ;
  Wells of unfathomed fire, and water-springs
  Whence the great sea, even as a child, is fed,
  Whose vapours clothe earth's monarch mountain-tops
  With kingly ermine-snow.   The beams flash on
  And make appear the melancholy ruins
  Of cancelled cycles—anchors, beaks of ships,
  Planks turned to marble, quivers, helms, and spears,
  And gorgon-headed targes, and the wheels
  Of scythèd chariots, and the emblazonry
  Of trophies, standards, and armorial beasts—
  Round which death laughed ; sepulchred emblems
  Of dead destruction, ruin within ruin !
  The wrecks beside of many a city vast
  Whose population which the earth grew over
  Was mortal, but not human : see, they lie,
  Their monstrous works and uncouth skeletons,
  Their statues, homes and fanes—prodigious shapes
  Huddled in grey annihilation, split,
  Jammed in the hard black deep ; and, over these,
  The anatomies of unknown wingèd things,
  And fishes which were isles of living scale,
  And serpents, bony chains, twisted around
  The iron crags, or within heaps of dust
  To which the tortuous strength of their last pangs
  Had crushed the iron crags ; and over these
  The jagged alligator, and the might
  Of earth-convulsing behemoth, which once
  Were monarch-beasts, and on the slimy shores
  And weed-overgrown continents of earth

> Increased and multiplied like summer-worms
> On an abandoned corpse, till the blue globe
> Wrapt deluge round it like a cloak, and they
> Yelled, gasped, and were abolished; or some God
> Whose throne was in a comet passed and cried
> ' Be not,' and, like my words, they were no more."

Passages in a different vein might be quoted, as these lines of apophthegm in the " Cenci : "—

> " In the great war between the young and old
> I, who have white hairs and a tottering body,
> Will keep at least blameless neutrality ; "

or this fine image :—

> " Life, like a dome of many-coloured glass,
> Stains the white radiance of eternity."

In some of the rougher political poems—as in the burlesque of *Œdipus Tyrannus,* and in *Peter Bell the Third*—there is even a kind of fierce popular wit, appealing to the coarsest understanding, and intended to do so. Nor is it necessary to refer to those shorter lyrical pieces, *The Sensitive Plant, The Cloud,* the *Ode to the Skylark,* &c., which are known even to those who know nothing else of Shelley, and read again and again for their melody,

> "Sweet as a singing rain of silver dew."

In others of these lyrical pieces what intensity of pathos ! Who that has ever heard Beatrice's wild song

in the "Cenci" sung as it should be can forget its
plaintive horror?—

> "False friend, wilt thou smile or weep
> 　When my life is laid asleep?
> 　Little cares for a smile or a tear
> 　The clay-cold corpse upon the bier.
> 　　　Farewell! Heigh ho!
> 　　　What is this whispers low?
> There's a snake in thy smile, my dear;
> And bitter poison within thy tear."

After all, however, less than almost any other poet,
is Shelley to be adequately represented in detached
passages. His poetry is like an intellectual ether, that
must be breathed and lived in for some time ere its
influence can be appreciated. To minds of sufficient
culture, who have in this way become acquainted with
Shelley's poetry (and only minds of considerable
culture are likely ever to read much of it), it has
always presented itself as something very peculiar in
quality—totally different, for example, from the poetry
of Milton, or of Wordsworth, or of Byron, or of any
other preceding poet. To this, at least, Shelley's poetry
can lay claim—that, whether great or not, whether
useful or hurtful in its influence, it is very peculiar.

Retaining for the nonce a distinction, somewhat pe-
dantic in form, and greatly laughed at of late by the
lovers of plain English (but which need not be given

up, for all that, till the lovers of plain English have
provided an exact equivalent), one cannot do better
than repeat the observation, often made already, that
Shelley belongs to the order of the so-called "subjective" poets, as differing from those called the
"objective." The terms do express a real meaning.
There are some poets—as, for example, Chaucer,
Shakespeare, and Scott—whose poetry consists, in the
main, of combinations, more or less complex, of scenery,
incident, and character, each fashioned by a kind of
wondrous craft out of materials furnished to the imagination by sense, memory, reading, and reflection, and
each, as soon as it is fashioned, detached altogether,
or nearly so, from the personality of the writer, and
sent to float away as a separate creation down the
stream of time. In the case of these so-called "objective" poets, it is a problem of the highest difficulty
to ascertain the personal character from their works.
Out of one set of materials Shakespeare fashions a
"Hamlet;" then he sets about a "Macbeth;" then
he betakes himself to a "Henry the Fourth," or a
"Midsummer Night's Dream;" but whether Shakespeare himself is most in one or in another of these
creations, is a matter not to be lightly determined on
mere internal evidence. We see those creations separately and successively issuing from Shakespeare's
mind, and we know that they were fashioned there by

a subtle craft operating upon materials that had been
brought into that mind from the surrounding world ;
but what kind of chamber that mind was—of what
glooms, griefs, or distractions it may have been the
scene while the labour of creation was going on in
it—the works themselves do not accurately inform us.
For fifty years the world is amazed and delighted with
gorgeous phantasies of colour, representing, as they
were never represented before in painting, the phases
of universal nature ; and, when these phantasies are
traced to their source, they are found to be from the
hand of a taciturn and slovenly old man, named
Turner, shambling about in his slippers in a dusty
cobwebby house in London, and reputed by those who
knew no better to be very gruff and very avaricious,
and to have apparently no other usual human taste
than a fondness for port wine. Of course, even in such
cases, independent knowledge of the man may enable
us to discern him in his works.   There *are*, moreover,
for critics profound enough in their investigations,
subtle laws connecting the imagination with the personality and the life. But any such ultimate connexion, discovered or discoverable, between the personal
character of the " objective " poet and the nature of
his creations is a far different thing from the obvious
relation subsisting between the character of the " subjective " poet and *his* phantasies.   Here we are never

at a loss. The poetry of the "subjective" poet is nothing else than an effluence from his personality through the medium of his imagination. He has certain fixed ideas, certain permanent moods of mind, certain notions as to what ought to be and what ought not to be ; and these ideas, moods, or notions, he works forth into all that he fancies. He preaches while he sings ; what he imagines is a revelation of what he wishes. He does not live in a house of stone (to use a figure which, I think, is Mr. Browning's), communicating only by certain chinks and embrasures with the world without, and in which the possessor, while commanding a prospect all round, may keep himself and his own movements concealed. He lives in a house of glass, expressing his feelings as to what he sees in gestures visible to all about him, and employing the poetic art only as a means of flashing his own image and its successive gesticulations to a greater and greater distance. Here too the means of the poetic art correspond with the intention. The "subjective" poet, the poet of fixed ideas—dealing, as it is his tendency to do, not with things as they are in their infinite real complexity, but with the supposed principles of things, the springs or seeds of being,—such a poet may frame his pictures out of the stuff of real life, if he chooses, just as the "objective" poet does ; but even then, owing to the invariable meaning which he infuses into

K

them, they will be in one strain, and more or less
repetitions of each other. In Byron's poetry, for
example, under very various forms, we have still a
reproduction of the Byronic type of character. On
the whole, however, it will be the tendency of the
"subjective" poet of the most determined type not to
take his scenery and circumstance from the real or
historical world at all—not to hamper himself with the
actual relations of time, place, and historical probability
—but, as he concerns himself morally with Man in
his primal elements, so to deal also with material
nature as simplified into its masses and generalizations.
In other words, he will lay his scene anywhere in
vague time or space; he will make his persons gigantic,
mythical, and featureless, and will unfetter the mode
of their actions from the ordinary terrestrial laws ;
and the objects amid which they move he will depict
as visual allegories. Hence that well-known deficiency
of human interest which often prevents poetry of this
kind from being widely popular. Most men like to
have their footing on a solid flooring of fact and
history, and do not take nearly so much pleasure in
a world of a few elemental ingredients and relations,
fashioned to illustrate the action of a few supposed
springs of being, as they do in representations of the
living and moving complexity of our own wrinkled
planet.

The distinction we have been expounding is, of
course, not absolute. It would be difficult to name a
poet belonging so purely to one of the orders as to
have nothing in him of the other. On the whole,
however, Shelley is eminently a "subjective" poet.
In his *Cenci,* his *Julian and Maddalo,* and one or two
other poems, he does make it his aim to represent
historical occurrences, and scenes and feelings as they
are found in actual life. But, in the main, he is a
poet of fixed ideas—a poet dealing incessantly with
the seeds and springs of being, and illustrating his
notions of these in imaginations of an arbitrary and
mythological character. His Poetry is, in fact, a kind
of air-hung Mythology, shadowing forth the essential
principles of a creed which might be called Shelleyism.
What this creed was we have already partly seen in
our sketch of his life; but a word or two more may
be added.

At one time Shelley had, as he tells us himself,
been a Materialist in philosophy. That is to say, he
regarded the universe as consisting of an original basis
or consolidation of matter of the kind called Inorganic,
upon which there had been reared, or out of which
there had somehow grown, a quantity of other and
more highly developed matter of the kind called
Organic, ascending in a hierarchy of forms, with Man

at the apex.   According to this philosophy, in thinking
of the universe, one is bound to think of matter and
of nothing else—matter lying dead and obdurate, or
matter pervaded by electricities, nerve-forces, and what
not, so as to be locomotive, sensitive, active, and reflective.   But this philosophy Shelley had soon and very
decidedly abandoned ; and, instead of it, he had taken
up what is called the system of Idealism.   According
to this philosophy—which he had got at through
Hume and Berkeley, and partly through Plato,—not
Matter, but Thought, is the fundamental reality of the
universe.   Everything is thought; nothing exists but
in and through thought.   What we call external
objects, what we call matter itself, is but thought of
a certain quantity and variety, distinguished from
thought recognised as such by certain accidents of
force, frequency, and the like.   Thoughts in certain
successions, and in certain degrees of intensity : that
is all we know anything of.   The universe is but
a certain coagulation or huge bubble-mountain of
thoughts—the harder and more coagulated parts of the
mass, crushed by the gravity of the others, constituting
what we call matter, and forming a permanent basis
for all ; and the rest ascending in successive stages
of tenuity till they end in the ether of once-imagined
whimsies.   But, this being the case, it follows that
the universe may be continually added to and disturbed

in its fabric. Thoughts being things, and the mind having the power of pouring forth a constant succession of new thoughts, these really rush into the fabric of the past accumulation, and, in adjusting themselves and finding their places, disturb its porosity, and keep it continually agitated. Above all, the poet, whose very business it is to send forth new imaginations of a great and impressive character, is thus always agitating, disturbing, and remodelling creation. This is a doctrine which Shelley is perpetually repeating in his prose-writings. " Imagination," he says, " or mind employed prophetically in imaging forth its objects, is the faculty of human nature on which every gradation of its progress—nay, every, the minutest, change—depends." According to Shelley, all the thoughts of all minds are adding to and altering the universe ; but it is the business of the poet, by certain splendid precalculated imaginations, either softly to disintegrate the mass of previously accumulated existence, so that it shall fall into new arrangements, or sometimes to convulse, crack, and rend this mass by the blast of a wholesome explosion through what was previously a chaos. The Poet would thus be pre-eminently the Reformer.

So far we have but the theoretical side of Shelley's system. The difficulty is to see how, when he had risen theoretically to the extreme of his Idealism, he

turned in mid-air, and came back on the world in a
scheme of practical reason. Admit the universe to
be a coagulation of old thoughts, modifiable by new
ones, what *kinds* of new thoughts will make the right
and desirable modification? What is the principle,
what the rule, what the right and wrong, in thought?
The poet, as the reformer-in-chief for the human race,
has to employ himself in splendid pre-calculated
imaginations, which, rushing forth from him, shall
softly arrange things in new harmonies, or violently
split their way with revolutionary force! Well,
wherein consists the splendour to be desired in these
imaginations, and on what principles are they to be
precalculated? Here, as is often the case with philosophers, there is a gap in which we cannot see the
links connecting Shelley's theoretical or ascending with
his practical or descending reason. But he *has* a
practical system, and a very definite one. Unlike
Hume, he ascends to the extreme of Idealism, not to
end in indifference or scepticism, but to descend again
all the more vehemently upon the world of man and
life, armed with a faith. He speaks, indeed, of Deity,
and other such ideas, as being only "the modes in
which thoughts are combined;" but it is evident, whatever he calls them, that it is only the presence or the
absence of certain ideas of this class that constitutes,
in his view, the difference between the right and the

wrong, between the splendid and the mean, in thought. Thoughts combined *so* are eternally noble and good; thoughts combined *otherwise* are eternally ignoble and bad—no man ever cherished a belief of this kind more passionately than Shelley. No man, therefore, had more of the essence of an absolute ethical faith, of a faith not fabricated out of experience, but structurally derived from an authority in the invisible. Theoretically an idealist, he was morally a fanatic. " I have confidence in my moral sense alone, for that is a kind of originality," is one of his own significant sayings. His whole life is an illustration. His brief existence in the world was one continued shriek about love and justice. He had "a passion," he says, "for reforming the world." Nor was it a superficial reform that he contemplated. From first to last, as he thought, human society had been an aggregate of wrong and corruption. Kings, priests, and governments had filled the earth with misery. Bound by sophisms and slavish fears, men and women were living defrauded of their natural rights, and out of their natural relations.

" Kings, priests, and statesmen blast the human flower
  Even in its tender bud ; their influence darts,
  Like subtle poison, through the bloodless veins
  Of desolate society."

But this state of things is not to last for ever ! There

will one day be a reign of truth and love, of justice
and social equality !

> " Spirit of Nature ! thou
> Life of interminable multitudes,
>> Soul of those mighty spheres
> Whose changeless paths through Heaven's deep
>> silence lie,
>> Soul of that smallest being
>>> The dwelling of whose life
>> Is one faint April sun-gleam—
>>> Man, like these passive things,
> Thy will unconsciously fulfilleth :
>> Like theirs, his age of endless peace,
>>> Which Time is fast maturing,
>>> Will swiftly, surely, come ;
> And the unbounded frame which thou pervadest
>> Will be without a flaw
> Marring its perfect symmetry."

This is Shelley's fixed faith, the burthen of all his
poetry.   It was his own aim as a poet to send forth
sounds that might shake the reign of " Anarch Custom,"
and hasten the blessed era in whose coming he believed.
Nor was it only on the great scale that he desired
to be a prophet of love and justice.   He was to carry
out his principle to its minutest applications, promoting
every movement for the mitigation of social or individual suffering, and so constituting himself, as well
in literature as in action, what nature, in framing him
so delicately, had fitted him to be—

> " A nerve o'er which might creep
> The else unfelt oppressions of this earth."

Here we recur to a question already opened. Whatever Shelley's formal affirmations respecting the doctrines of Deity and Immortality might be, it is clear that the fanatical intensity of his ethical creed implied a habit of viewing the world from a point out of itself, and by the rule of ideas not belonging to it. Had his principle been " to apprehend no farther than this world," why such spasm, why such wailing, such rage against universal wrong, such frantic longing to re-fashion human nature from its very roots? On such a principle, it is true, a man might be so far a reformer. He might seek to correct the earth by itself, the part by the knowledge of the whole, social evils in Asia by the experience of Europe. But for a man to start up and proclaim the whole past movement of humanity to have been wrong, and to propose to arrest it, and shift its very wheels, is a different matter. This was Shelley's proposition. He did not propose only that the world should be corrected by itself, the part by the whole, but that it should be corrected by a rule eternal and immutable, which he sometimes called love or justice, and sometimes the spirit of universal nature. There *was* a Heart beating somewhere, to whose pulsations the earth as a whole was rebel, but which would yet subdue the earth to unison with it; and, meanwhile, the agents of

good and the harbingers of the final harmony were to
be those imaginations of man which, by relating themselves to this Heart, were to be prematurely in unison
with it, and at war with the earth and its customs.
Nothing short of this belief, however he phrased it,
was the principle of Shelley's practical philosophy.
Seeing that it was so, might not we say that, like his
own Prometheus, he had tipped his reed with stolen
fire?

Argument and metaphysics apart, there is, at least,
no way in which the *fancy* may more easily apprehend
the peculiarity of Shelley's genius than by thinking of
him as one who surveyed the world not from a point
within it or on it, but from a point in distant space.
Better still, perhaps, one might think of him as not a
native of the earth at all, but some fluttering spirit of
a lighter sphere, that had dropped on the earth by
chance, unable to be in happy relation to it as a whole,
though keenly sensitive to some of its beauties. Were
our science of pedigree worth anything, it might save
us the necessity of any such figure. Remembering
that the year of Shelley's birth was that of the utmost
agony of the French Revolution, when convulsion was
shaking all things established, and new social principles
were everywhere abroad, we might then have a glimmering how it happened that the genius of the time
took a whim to appear even in Sussex, and bespeak as

one of its incarnations the child of a commonplace English baronet, who had never bargained for such an honour. But, unable to make anything to the purpose of such a scientific fancy, we may resort to the other. Shelley's personal friends used to resort to it. " I used to tell him," says Leigh Hunt, "that he had come from the planet Mercury." One may vary the form of the fancy; and, though the pale planet Mercury, the sickly darling of the sun, seems such an orb as Shelley might have come from, had he come from any, it might be fitter to fancy that he had come from none, but, till till he touched our earth, had been winging about in unsubstantial ether. When Milton's rebel host left the celestial realms, angels flocking on angels and the great Archangel leading, might we not suppose that some small seraph, who had joined the rebellion, lagged behind the rest in his flight, became detached from them by regret or weakness, and, unable to overtake them, was left to flutter disconsolate and alone amid the starry spaces? Excluded from Heaven, but not borne down with the rest into Pandemonium, if this creature did at last come near our orb in his wanderings, might it not become his refuge; and then might we not suppose that, though retaining the principle of rebellion—so that, when the Highest was named, he would shriek against the name—yet his recollections of his original would be purer, and his nature less impaired, than if, instead of transparent space, populous Pandemonium had been his intermediate home ?

Whatever form we give to the fancy, the characteristics of Shelley's poetry are such as to accord with it. Intense as is his ethical spirit, his desire to act upon man and society, his imagination cannot work with things as he finds them, with the actual stuff of historical life. His mode of thinking is not according to the terrestrial conditions of time, place, cause and effect, variety of race, climate, and costume. His persons are shapes, winged forms, modernized versions of Grecian mythology, or mortals highly allegorized; and their movements are vague, swift, and independent of ordinary physical laws. In the *Revolt of Islam*, for example, the story is that of two lovers who career through the plains and cities of an imaginary kingdom on a Tartar horse, or skim over leagues of ocean in a boat whose prow is of moonstone. But for the *Cenci*, and one or two other pieces, one would say that Shelley had scarcely any aptitude for the historical. Even in his sensuous imagery the same arbitrariness is apparent. His landscapes, like his persons, are a sort of allegories. His true poetical element, where alone he takes things as he finds them, is the atmosphere. Shelley is preeminently the poet of what may be called meteorological circumstance. He is at home among winds, mists, rains, snows, clouds gorgeous-

ly coloured, glories of sunrise, nights of moonshine,
lightnings, streamers, and falling stars; and what of
vegetation and geology he brings in is but as so much
that might be seen by an aerial creature in its ascents
and descents. His poetry is full of direct and all but
conscious suggestions of this. Need we cite, as one,
his *Ode to the Skylark*, that "scorner of the ground,"
whose skill he covets for the poet? Then there is his
lyric of *The Cloud*:—

> " I bring fresh showers for the thirsting flowers,
>   For the seas and the streams;
> I bear light shade for the leaves when laid
>   In their noon-day dreams;
> From my wings are shaken the dews that waken
>   The sweet birds every one,
> When rocked to rest on their mother's breast
>   As she dances about the sun;
> I wield the flail of the lashing hail,
>   And whiten the green plains under,
> And then again I dissolve in rain,
>   And laugh as I pass in thunder."

Again in his *Invocation to the West Wind*, in which,
expressly imploring it to be *his* spirit, he dedicates
himself, as it were, to the meteorological for ever:—

> " O wild West Wind, thou breath of Autumn's being,
> Thou from whose unseen presence the leaves dead
> Are driven, like ghosts from an enchanter fleeing,
>   *   *   *   *   *   *
> Make me thy lyre, even as the forest is!

What if my leaves are falling like its own?
The tumult of thy mighty harmonies

Will take from both a deep autumnal tone,
Sweet though in sadness.　Be thou, spirit fierce,
My spirit!　Be thou *me*, impetuous one!

Drive my dead thoughts over the universe,
Like withered leaves, to quicken a new birth;
And, by the incantation of this verse,

Scatter, as from an unextinguished hearth
Ashes and sparks, my words among mankind!
Be through my lips to unawakened earth

The trumpet of a prophecy!　O wind,
If Winter comes, can Spring be far behind?

IV.

THE LIFE AND POETRY OF KEATS.

IV.

THE LIFE AND POETRY OF KEATS.[1]

KEATS was born in Moorfields, London, in October 1795, the son of a livery-stable keeper of some wealth, who had attained that position by marrying his master's daughter and so succeeding him in the business. There were five children, four sons and a daughter, of whom John was the third. The father, who is described as an active, energetic little man of much natural talent, was killed by a fall from a horse at the age of thirty-six, when Keats was in his ninth year ; and the care of the children devolved upon the mother, a tall, large-featured woman, of considerable force of character. There was also a maternal uncle, a very tall, strong, and courageous man, who had been in the navy, had served under Duncan at Camperdown, and had done extraordinary feats in the way of fighting. Partly in emulation of this uncle, partly

[1] *Macmillan's Magazine,* November 1860.

from constitutional inclination, the boys were always
fighting too—in the house, about the stables, or out
in the adjacent streets, with each other, or with any-
body else.   John, though the shortest for his years,
and the most like his father, was the most pugnacious
of the lot; but with his pugnacity he combined, it is
said, a remarkable sensibility, and a great love of fun.
This character he took with him to a boarding-school
at Enfield, near London, kept by the father of Mr.
Charles Cowden Clarke, then also a boy, not much
older than Keats, receiving his education under his
father's roof.   At school, Keats, according to the
recollections of Mr. Clarke and others of his school-
fellows, was at first a perfect little terrier for resolute-
ness and pugnacity, but very placable and frolicsome,
very much liked, and, though not particularly studious,
very quick at learning.   There would seem to have
been more of pleasant sociability between the family
of the master and the scholars in the school at Enfield,
and more of literary talk at bye-hours, than were then
common at private English schools.   At all events,
when, by the death of his mother, of lingering consumption, in 1810, the guardianship of Keats, his two
surviving brothers, and his only sister, devolved on a
Mr. Abbey, a London merchant who had known the
family, and when Mr. Abbey thought it best to take
two of the boys from school and apprentice them to

professions, it was felt by Keats to be a very happy
arrangement that he was apprenticed to a surgeon-
apothecary at Edmonton, so near to Enfield that he
could still go over when he liked to see the Clarkes.
He was then fifteen years of age. His share of the
family property, held for him by his guardian till he
came of age, was about 2,000*l.*; and his apprenticeship
was to last five years.

From Edmonton Keats was continually walking over
to Enfield to see his young friend, Cowden Clarke,
and to borrow books. It was some time in 1812 that
he borrowed Spenser's *Faery Queene.* The effect was
immediate and extraordinary. "He ramped," says
Mr. Clarke, "through the scenes of the romance;"
he would talk of nothing but Spenser; he had whole
passages by heart, which he would repeat; and he
would dwell with an ecstasy of delight on fine particular phrases, such as "the sea-shouldering whale."
His first known poetical composition (he was then
seventeen) was a piece expressly entitled "In Imitation of Spenser."

> "Now Morning from her orient chamber came,
>   And her first footsteps touch'd a verdant hill,
>   Crowning its lawny crest with amber flame,
>   Silvering the untainted gushes of its rill;
>   Which, pure from mossy beds," &c.

From that moment it seemed as if Keats lived only

to read poetry and to write it. From Spenser he went to Chaucer, from Chaucer to Milton, and so on and on, with ever-widening range, through all our sweeter and greater poets. He luxuriated in them by himself; he talked about them, and read parts of them aloud to his friends; he became a critic of their thoughts, their words, their rhymes, their cadences. His chief partner in these tastes was Mr. Cowden Clarke, with whom he would take walks, or sit up whole evenings, discoursing of poets and poetry; and he acknowledges, in one of his metrical epistles, the influence which Mr. Clarke had in forming his literary likings. Above all, it was Mr. Clarke that first introduced him to any knowledge of ancient Greek poetry. This was effected by lending him Chapman's Homer, his first acquaintance with which, and its effects on him, are celebrated in one of the finest and best-known of his sonnets. Thenceforward Greek poetry, so far as it was accessible to him in translation, had peculiar fascinations for him. By similar means he became fondly familiar with some of the softer Italian poets, and with the stories of Boccaccio. It was noted by one of his friends that his preferences at this time, whether in English or in other poetry, were still for passages of sweet, sensuous description, or of sensuous-ideal beauty, such as are to be found in the minor poems of Milton, Shakespeare and Chaucer, and in Spenser throughout, and that he rarely seemed to dwell with the same enthusiasm on passages of fervid feeling, of severe reference to life, or of powerful human interest. At this time, in fact, his feeling for poetry was very much that of an artist in language, observing effects which particularly delighted him, and studying them with a professional admiration of the exquisite. He brooded over fine phrases like a lover; and often, when he met a quaint or delicious word in the course of his reading, he would take pains to make it his own by using it, as speedily as possible, in some poem he was writing. Ah! those days of genial, enjoying youth, when, over the fire, with a book in one's hand, one got fine passages by heart, and, in walks with one or two choice companions, there was an opening of the common stock, and hours and miles were whiled away with tit-bits of recent reading from a round of favourite poets! Those were the days when books were books; and it is a fact to be remembered, as regards literature, that one half of the human race is always under the age of twenty-one.

Before Keats's apprenticeship was over, it was pretty clear to himself and his friends that he would not persevere in becoming a surgeon. In the year 1816, when he came from Edmonton to London, at the age of twenty, he did indeed enter himself as a student at the hospitals; but he very soon gave up attending

them, and found more agreeable employment in the
society of Leigh Hunt, Shelley, Godwin, Dilke, Ollier,
the painter Haydon, Hazlitt, Charles Armitage Brown,
and others whose names are less remembered.   In this
society of artists and men of letters—forming, so far
as the literary ingredient was concerned, the so-called
" Cockney School," as distinct from the " Lakists " of
the North of England, and from the Edinburgh men
who gave both of them their names—Keats at once
took a prominent place, less on account of what he
had actually done than on the promise of what he
was to be.   On first settling in London, he had taken
lodgings in the Poultry, in the heart of the City; but,
as soon as he had abandoned the idea of following
the medical profession, he removed to Hampstead, a
suburb of London as you approach it from the north.

London, with all the evils resulting from its vast-
ness, has suburbs as rich and beautiful, after the
English style of scenery, as any in the world ; and
even now, despite the encroachments of the ever-
encroaching brick and mortar on the surrounding
country, the neighbourhood of Hampstead and Highgate, near London, is one in which the lover of
natural beauty and the solitary might well delight.
The ground is much the highest round London ; there
are real heights and hollows, so that the omnibuses

coming from town have to put on additional horses;
you ascend steep roads, lying in part through villages
of quaint shops, and old, high-gabled brick houses,
still distinct from the great city, though about to be
devoured by it—in part through straggling lines of
villas, with gardens and grassy parks round them,
and here and there an old inn; and, from the highest
eminences, when the view is clear, you can see London
left behind, a mass of purplish mist, with domes and
steeples visible through it. Where the villages end,
you are really in the country. There is the Heath,
on the Hampstead side—an extensive tract of knolls
and little glens, covered here and there with furze,
all abloom with yellow in the summer, when the
larks may be heard singing over it; threaded here
and there by paths with seats in them, or broken by
clumps of trees, and blue rusty-nailed palings, which
enclose old-fashioned family-houses and shrubberies,
where the coachman in livery may be seen talking
lazily to the gardener; but containing also sequestered spots where one might wander alone for hours,
or lie concealed amid the sheltering furze. At night,
Hampstead Heath would be as ghastly a place to
wander in as an uneasy spirit could desire. In every
hollow, seen in the starlight, one could fancy that
there had been a murder; nay, tradition points to
spots where foul crimes have been committed, or

where, in the dead of night, forgers, who had walked,
with discovery on their track, along dark intervening
roads, from the hell of lamp-lit London, had lain
down and poisoned themselves. In the day, however,
and especially on a bright summer day, the scene is
open, healthy, and cheerful. On the one side, is a
view across a green valley, called "The Vale of
Health," to the opposite heights of Highgate; on the
other, the eye traverses a flat expanse of fields and
meadows, stretching for many miles northward, and
looking, in its rich level variety, like a miniature
representation of all England. And then the lanes
all about and around, leading away from the Heath,
deep and steep, between high banks and along the
old church and churchyard, and past little ponds and
gardens, and often ending in footpaths through fields,
where one has to get over stiles !

All this of Hampstead and its vicinity even now
[1860]; but, forty years ago, it was still better. At
that time London itself was a different city. There
was less smoke; there were no steamers on the river;
and from the overspanning bridges the water could be
seen running clear beneath, with the consciousness of
fish in it. Then, too, the conveyance between London
and such suburbs as Hampstead and Highgate was
not by omnibuses passing every five minutes, but by
the old stage-coaches, with their guards and horns,

coming and going leisurely twice or thrice a day. In those days, therefore, Hampstead and Highgate were still capable of having an individuality of their own, and of having associations fixed upon them by the occupations of their residents, even though these were in London daily, and were, by their general designation, properly enough, Londoners. Part of their celebrity now, indeed, arises from associations thus formed. Old Leigh Hunt, visiting those scenes not long before his death, would point out the exact wooden seat on the Heath where he and Keats, or where he and Shelley, sat when such and such a poem was recited, or the exact spot in a path through the fields where Coleridge took leave of him and Charles Lamb, to dawdle back to his home at Highgate, and where Lamb, while the departing skirts of the sage were visible, stuttered out some pun about his personal appearance and his last metaphysical monologue. At the particular time of which we are now speaking Leigh Hunt was living at Hampstead, where also lived Mr. Armitage Brown, a retired merchant of literary tastes, and others of whom it is not necessary to take note; and there, in the evenings, at the houses of such men, artists and others would drop in; and then, O ye future critics of *Blackwood* and the *Quarterly*, what wit there would be, what music, what portfolios of sketches and engravings, what white casts from the antique, what talk about poetry and literature! From that time, with scarcely an exception, Hampstead was the London home of Keats— first as a guest of Leigh Hunt, or a lodger near to him; and afterwards, and more permanently, as a guest of Mr. Armitage Brown. Indeed, just as Wordsworth and his associates were supposed to have constituted themselves into a school by retiring to Cumberland and Westmoreland, in order to be in closer relations to nature, as exhibited in that district of lake and mountain, so it might have been suggested maliciously of Keats, Hunt, and the rest of their set, that the difference between them and the elder school was that what *they* called Nature was Nature as seen from Hampstead Heath. As the one set of poets had received from their Edinburgh critics the name of "the Lakists," so, to make the joke correspond, the others, instead of being called "the Cockney Poets," might have been named the Hampstead Heath-ens.

Keats signalized his accession to this peculiar literary group by publishing, in 1817, a little volume of poems, containing some of his sonnets and other pieces now appended to his longer and later compositions. The volume scarcely touched the attention of the public, though it served to show his power to his immediate friends. He was then two-and-twenty years of age; and his appearance was rather singular. Coleridge, who once shook hands with him, when he met him with Hunt in a lane near Highgate, describes him as "a loose, slack, not well-dressed youth." The descriptions of Hunt and others are more particular. He was considerably under middle height, his lower limbs being small, in comparison with the upper, to a degree that marred his whole proportion. His shoulders were very broad for his size; his face was strongly cut, yet delicately mobile, expressing an un-usual combination of determination with sensibility, its worst feature being the mouth, which had a pro-jecting upper lip, and altogether a savage pugilistic look. Nor did the look belie him. He had great personal courage, and once took the trouble to thrash a butcher for some insolent conduct in a regular stand-up fight. His hair was brown, and his eyes large, and of a dark, glowing blue. "His head," says Leigh Hunt, "was a puzzle for the phrenologists, "being remarkably small in the skull—a singularity "which he had in common with Byron and Shelley, "whose hats I could not get on." His voice, unlike Shelley's, was deep and grave. His entire expres-sion was that of eager power; and, in contradiction of what was observed of him at an earlier period, he was now easily, though still apparently against his will, betrayed into signs of vehement emotion. "At the recital of a noble action, or a beautiful thought," says Mr. Hunt, "his eyes would suffuse with tears, and his mouth trembled." On hearing of some unmanly conduct, he once burst out, "Why is there not a human dust-hole into which to tumble such fellows?" Evidently ill-health, as well as imaginative temperament, had to do with this inability to restrain tears and other signs of agitated feeling. His mother had died of consumption at a comparatively early age; his younger brother, Tom, was already far gone in the same fatal malady; and, though there was as yet no distinct symptom of consumption in Keats, he was often flushed and feverish, and had his secret fears. He had many hours of sprightliness, however, when those fears would vanish, and he would be full of frolic and life. In allusion to this occasional excess of fun and animal spirits, his friends punned upon his name, shortening it from "John Keats" into "Junkets." Still, amid all—in his times of despondency, as well as in his seasons of hope—Poetry was his ceaseless thought, and to be a Poet his one ambition :—

> " O for ten years, that I may overwhelm
>   Myself in Poesy ! So I may do the deed
>   That my own soul has to itself decreed ! "

Of what *kind* this intended deed was we have also some indication. Like all the fresher young poets of his time, Keats had imbibed, partly from constitutional predisposition, partly from conscious reasoning, that theory of Poetry which, for more than twenty years, Wordsworth had been disseminating by precept and by example through the literary mind of England. This theory, in its historical aspect, I will venture to call *Pre-Drydenism.* Its doctrine, historically, was that the age of true English Poetry was the period anterior to Dryden—the period of Chaucer, Spenser, Shakespeare, Fletcher, and Milton—and that, with a few exceptions, the subsequent period, from Dryden inclusively down to the time of Wordsworth's own appearance as a poet, had been a prosaic interregnum, during which what passed for poetry was either an inflated style of diction which custom had rendered pleasing, or, at best, shrewd sense and wit, or miscellaneous cogitation, more or less weighty, put into metre.

Take an example. Here are two stanzas from a well-known paraphrase of Scripture, still sung in churches over a large part of the kingdom.

> " In life's gay morn, when sprightly youth
>   With vital ardour glows,
>   And shines in all the fairest charms
>   Which beauty can disclose,

Deep on thy soul, before its powers
   Are yet by vice enslaved,
Be thy Creator's glorious name
   And character engraved."

How remorselessly Wordsworth would have torn this
passage to pieces—as, indeed, he did a similar paraphrase of Scripture by Dr. Johnson! · "Life's gay
morn!" "sprightly youth!" he would have said,—
meaningless expressions, used because it is considered
poetical to stick an adjective before every noun, and
"gay" and "sprightly" are adjectives conveniently in
stock! Then, "sprightly youth with vital ardour
glows"—what is this but slip-shod; and, besides, why
tug the verb to the end of the phrase and say "with
vital ardour glows," instead of "glows with vital
ardour," as you would do in natural speech? O,
of course, the rhyme! Yes; but who asked you
to rhyme at all, in the first place? and, in the
next place, if you were bent on rhyming, and found
"ardour" would not suit at the end of your precious line, that was *your* difficulty, not mine! What
are you a poet for but to overcome such difficul-
ties, or what right have you to extract the rhythms
and rhymes that you want in your craft as a versifier from the mere torture of honest prose? And
then, worse and worse, "Youth," already "glowing,"
with this "vital ardour," also, it seems, "shines,"

and (marvellous metaphor!) shines "with charms"—
which "charms" (metaphor still more helpless!) are
"the fairest charms disclosed by beauty!" And so
on he would have gone, pointing out the flaws of
meaning and of expression in the next stanza in the
same stern manner. Pass, he would have said at last,
from this poor jingle of words to the simple and
beautiful text of which it is offered as a paraphrase:
"Remember now thy Creator in the days of thy
youth, while the evil days come not, nor the years
draw nigh, when thou shalt say, I have no pleasure
in them." The defects, he would have continued, seen
on a small scale in the foregoing metrical version of
this passage, were visible throughout the whole course
of English poetry after Milton—with here and there,
as in Thomson and Dyer, a remarkable exception.
There was then no faithfulness to fact in description
or in imagery from nature, no natural speech in verse,
nothing save more or less of intellectual vigour exhibited through an artificial form of diction, to which
men had grown so accustomed that they had ceased
to inspect it logically. Even men of real genius,
such as Dryden himself and Pope, were, in the bulk
of their writings, but splendid practitioners of a false
style, which, when people had been educated to see
its viciousness, would mar their fame as poets.

I am not here *discussing* Wordsworth's theory: I

am only *stating* it. Keats, I repeat, had adopted this theory, if not in all its particulars, at least in its essence. Thus, in one of his pieces, after speaking of the greatness of his old favourite English poets, he says—

" Could all this be forgotten ?   Yes, a schism
　Nurtured by foppery and barbarism
　Made great Apollo blush for this his land.
　Men were thought wise who could not understand
　His glories : with a puling infant's force
　They sway'd about upon a rocking-horse
　And thought it Pegasus.   Ah, dismal-soul'd !
　The winds of heaven blew, the ocean roll'd
　Its gathering waves ;—ye felt it not.   The blue
　Bared its eternal bosom, and the dew
　Of summer-night collected still to make
　The morning precious; Beauty was awake !
　Why were *ye* not awake ?   But ye were dead
　To things ye knew not of,—were closely wed
　To musty laws, lined out with wretched rule
　And compass vile ; so that ye taught a school
　Of dolts to smoothe, inlay, and clip and fit,
　Till, like the certain wands of Jacob's wit,
　Their verses tallied.   Easy was the task :
　A thousand handicraftsmen wore the mask
　Of poesy.   Ill-fated, impious race !
　That blasphemed the bright Lyrist to his face,
　And did not know it !   No, they went about,
　Holding a poor decrepit standard out,
　Mark'd with most flimsy mottoes, and, in large,
　The name of one Boileau !'"

Keats, then, was a Pre-Drydenist in his notions of poetry, and in his own intentions as a poetic artist. But I will say more. Wordsworth had then so far conquered the opposition through which he had been struggling that a modified Pre-Drydenism was universally diffused through English literary society, and the so-called Cockney, or Hampstead-Heath School, with whom accident had associated Keats, were largely tinged with it. They did not, indeed, go all the length with Wordsworth in depreciating Dryden and Pope (as who could?); but a superior relish for the older poets was one of their avowed characteristics. But in this, I believe, Keats went beyond the rest of them. It may be perceived, I think, that, with all his esteem for Hunt and Shelley, both as kind personal friends and as poets, he had notions respecting himself which led him, even while in their society and accounted one of them, to fix his gaze with steadier reverence than they did on the distant veteran of Rydal Mount. To Wordsworth alone does he seem to have looked as, all in all, a sublimity among contemporary poets.

So far, however, as Keats had yet been publicly heard of, it was only as one fledgling more in the brood of poets whose verses were praised in the *Examiner*. The things he had yet published were but little studies in language and versification, preparatory

M

to something that could be called a poem. Such a
poem he now resolved to write. Always drawn by
a kind of mental affinity to the sensuous Mythology
of the Greeks, he had chosen for his subject the
legend of Endymion, the youthful lover of the moon-
goddess Artemis. "A long poem," he said, "is the
test of invention ; and it will be a test of my invention if I can make 4,000 lines out of this one bare
circumstance, and fill them with poetry." To accom-
plish his task, he left London in the spring of 1817,
and took up his abode first in the Isle of Wight, then
at Margate (in both of which places he revelled in
the views of the sea as a newly-found pleasure), and
then, successively, at Canterbury, Oxford, and other
places inland. In the winter of 1817–18 he returned
to Hampstead with the four books of his *Endymion*
completed. The absence of seven or eight months,
during which this poem was written, was also
the period in which many of those letters to his
friends were written that have been edited by Mr.
Monckton Milnes, in his Memoir of the poet. These
letters have hardly received the attention they deserve.
They are very remarkable letters. One can see, indeed,
that they are the letters of an intellectual invalid, of
a poor youth too conscious of "the endeavour of this
present breath," watching incessantly his own morbid
symptoms, and communicating them to his friends.

There is also in them a somewhat unnatural straining after quaint and facetious conceits, as if he would not write common-place, but would force himself by the mere brief rumination of the moment into some minute originality or whim of fancy. On the whole, however, with the proper allowance, the letters may be read without any injury to the highest notion of him that may be formed from his compositions that were meant for publication; and there have not been many young poets of whose casual letters as much could be said. They abound in shrewd observations, in delicate and subtle criticisms, in fine touches of description, and in thoughts of a philosophical kind that are at once comprehensive and deep.

"*Endymion : A Poetic Romance*" appeared in the beginning of 1818. Its reception was not wholly satisfactory. It made Keats's name more widely known; it procured him visits and invitations; and, when he attended Hazlitt's lectures, ladies to whom he was pointed out looked at him instead of listening to the lecturer. But Hunt, Shelley, and the rest, though they admired the poem, and thought some passages in it very wonderful, had many faults to find. The language in many parts was juvenile, not to say untasteful; such phrases as "honey-feel of bliss" were too frequent; it was impossible for any understanding of a rational sort

M 2

to reconcile itself to such a bewildering plenitude of luxuriant invention raised on such a mere nothing of a basis ; and, on the whole, there was too evident a waywardness in the sequence of the thoughts, arising from a passive dependence of the matter at every point on the mere suggestion of the rhyme ! These and other such objections were heard on all hands. Worst of all, Wordsworth had no approbation to give. At Haydon's, one evening, when Wordsworth was present, Keats was induced to repeat to him the famous Hymn to Pan, which Shelley had praised as that in the whole poem which "gave the surest sign of ultimate excellence." The iron-grey poet heard it to the end, and then only remarked that it was "a pretty piece of paganism." And so, with no more encouragement than usually falls to the lot of a young man in such cases, Keats had to keep his own counsel, and look forward to other works, in which, choosing more solid subjects, he should exert his powers more compactly and impressively, and win, by better-disciplined strokes, the recognition which the world yields so slowly to forms of genius differing from those to which it has been accustomed. His was certainly a new faculty, which had to create and educate the taste by which it should itself be appreciated ; and his hope, therefore, lay with the body of the growing youth of the land, whose perpetual privilege it is that they alone can receive and enjoy without criticising. No man was ever fully and heartily accepted, among his own sex, except by those younger than himself.

Keats, there is no doubt, was prepared to wait and work on. The story of his having been killed by the savage article in the *Quarterly* is proved to have been wholly untrue. He had sense enough and courage enough to get over that chagrin within the usual period of twenty-four hours, which, if there is any use for human spirits in the earth's rotation, ought to bring them as well as other things round again to the *status quo*. But other causes were at work, some of which are but dimly revealed by his biographer, but the chief of which was his hereditary malady of consumption. In the winter of 1819–20 he was seized with the fatal blood-spitting he had long dreaded; after a few months of lingering, during which he seemed partly to fight with Death as one to whom life was precious, partly to long to die as one who had nothing to live for, he was removed to Italy; and there, having suffered much, he breathed his last at Rome on the 23d of February, 1821, at the age of twenty-five years and four months. He had wished for "ten years" of poetic life, but not half that term had been allowed him. The sole literary event of his life, after the publication of his *Endymion* in 1818, had been the publication of his *Lamia, The Eve of St. Agnes, and Other Poems*, in 1820; and the sole variation of his manner of life had consisted in his leaving Hampstead for a ramble or a residence in the country, and returning again from the country to Hampstead or London.

After all, whether a man is a poet, a philosopher, or a man of action, there *is* a common standard by which he may be tried, so as to measure his relative intellectual importance. The determination of this standard is difficult; but ultimately, I believe, the truest measure of every man, in intellectual respects, is the measure of his speculative or purely philosophical faculty. So far as this may be demurred to, the objection will arise, I fancy, from the practical difficulty of applying the test. It is only certain poets that give us the opportunity of judging of the strength of their rational or purely *noetic* organ—that faculty by which men speculate, or frame what are called "thoughts" or "propositions." Whenever this is done, however, then, *cæteris paribus*, the deeper thinker is the greater poet. Hence it is an excellent thing for the critic to catch his poet writing prose. He has him then at his mercy; he can keep him in the trap, and study him through the bars at his leisure. If he is a poor creature, he will be found out; if he has genuine vigour, then, with all allowance for any ungainliness arising from his being out of his proper element, there will be evidences of it. Now, tried by any test of this kind,

Keats will be found to have been no weakling. The
following passages from his prose letters, for example,
are, I believe, thoughts of pith and substance, whether
absolutely true or not:—

" Men of Genius are great as certain ethereal
chemicals operating on the mass of neutral intellect,
but they have not any individuality, any determined
character. I would call the top and head of those
who have a proper self Men of Power."

" Men should bear with each other; there is not the
man who may not be cut up, ay, lashed to pieces, on
his weakest side. The best of men have but a portion
of good in them—a kind of spiritual yeast in their
frames which creates the ferment of existence—by
which a man is propelled to act and strive and buffet
with circumstance. The sure way is, first to know a
man's faults, and then be passive. If, after that, he
insensibly draws you towards him, then you have no
power to break the link."

" I had, not a dispute, but a disquisition, with Dilke
upon various subjects. Several things dovetailed in
my mind, and at once it struck me what quality went
to form a man of achievement, especially in literature,
and which Shakespeare possessed so enormously—I
mean *negative capability;* that is, when a man is capable of being in uncertainties, mysteries, doubts,
without any irritable reaching after fact and reason.
. .. . This, pursued through volumes, would perhaps
take us no farther than this—that, with a great poet,
the sense of beauty overcomes every other consideration, or rather obliterates every other consideration."

" An extensive knowledge is necessary to thinking
people : it takes away the heat and fever, and helps,
by widening speculation, to ease the burden of the
mystery."

" Axioms in philosophy are not axioms till they have
been proved upon our pulses."

" I compare human life to a large mansion of many
apartments; two of which only I can describe—the
doors of the rest being as yet shut upon me. The
first we step into we call the Infant or Thoughtless
Chamber; in which we remain as long as we do not
think. We remain there a long while, and, notwithstanding the doors of the second chamber remain wide
open, showing a bright appearance, we care not to
hasten to it, but are imperceptibly impelled by the
awakening of the thinking principle within us. We
no sooner get into the second chamber, which I shall
call the Chamber of Maiden Thought, than we become
intoxicated with the light and the atmosphere. We
see nothing but pleasant wonders, and think of delaying there for ever in delight. However, among the
effects this breathing is father of, is that tremendous
one of sharpening one's vision into the heart and
nature of man, of convincing one's nerves that the
world is full of misery and heart-break, pain, sickness,
and oppression; whereby this Chamber of Maiden
Thought becomes gradually darkened, and, at the same
time, on all sides of it, many doors are set open, but all
dark—all leading to dark passages. We see not the
balance of good and evil; we are in a mist; we feel
the ' Burden of the Mystery.' To this point was
Wordsworth come, as far as I can conceive, when he
wrote *Tintern Abbey :* and it seems to me that his

genius is explorative of those dark passages. Now,
if we live and go on thinking, we too shall explore
them. He is a genius, and superior to us in so far as
he can, more than we, make discoveries, and shed a
light on them."

As the aphorisms and casual spurts of speculation
of a youth of twenty-two (and all the passages I
have quoted are from letters of his written before his
twenty-third year), these, I think, are sufficient proof
that Keats had an intellect from which his superiority
in some literary walk or other might have been surely
anticipated.

What we independently know enables us to say
that it was pre-eminently as a poet that he was fitted
to be distinguished. He was constitutionally a poet,
one of those minds in whom, to speak generally,
Imagination or Ideality is the sovereign faculty. But,
as we had occasion to explain in the paper on
Shelley, there are two recognised orders of poets,
each of which has its representatives in our literature
—that order, called "subjective," to which Shelley
himself belonged, and whose peculiarity it is that
their poems are vehicles for certain fixed ideas lying
in the minds of their authors, outbursts of their personal character, impersonations under shifting guises
of their wishes, feelings and beliefs; and that order,
on the other hand, distinguished as "objective," who

simply fashion their creations by a kind of inventive
craft working amid materials supplied by sense,
memory, and reading, without the distinct infusion
of any element of personal opinion. To this latter
order, as I said, belong Chaucer, Shakespeare, and
Scott. Now, indubitably, Keats, by the bulk of his
poetry, belongs to this order too. The contrast between him and Shelley, in this respect, is complete.
Contemporaries and friends, they were poets of quite
opposite schools and tendencies; and, so far as they
were repelled by each other's poetry (which they
were to a certain extent, despite their friendship), it
arose from this circumstance. Unlike the feminine
and ethereal Shelley, whose whole life was a shrill
supernatural shriek in behalf of certain principles,
Keats was a slack, slouching youth, with a thick
torso, a deep grave voice, and no fixed principles.
He had, as we have seen, his passing spurts of
speculation, but he had no system of philosophy.
So far as religious belief was concerned, he had no
wish to disturb existing opinions and institutions,
partly because he had really no such quarrel with
them as Shelley had, partly because he had no confidence in his ability to dogmatise on such points. In
politics, away from his personal connections, he was
rather conservative than otherwise. He thought the
Liverpool-and-Castlereagh policy very bad and oppres-

sive; but he did not expect that his friends, the
Liberals, would bring things very much nearer to the
millennium; and he distinctly avows that he was not,
like some of his friends, a Godwin-perfectibility man,
or an admirer of America as an advance beyond
Europe. In short, he kept aloof from opinion, doctrine, controversy, as by a natural instinct; he was
most at home in the world of sense and imagery,
where it was his pleasure to weave forth phantasies;
and, if his intelligence did now and then indulge in
a discursive flight, it was but by way of exercise, or
because opinions, doctrines, and controversies may be
considered as facts, and therefore as materials to be
worked into poetic language.

In quoting from Keats's letters I have purposely
selected passages showing that such was not only his
practice, but also his theory. His very principle of
poetry, it will be observed, almost amounts to this,
that the poet should have no principles. The distinction he makes between men of genius and men
of power is that the action of the former is like that
of an ethereal chemical, a subtle imponderable, passing
forth on diverse materials and rousing their affinities,
whereas the latter impress by their solid individuality.
So, again, when he speaks of the quality that forms
men for great literary achievement as being what he
calls a "negative capability"—a power of remaining,

and, as it were, luxuriously lolling, in doubts, mysteries, and half-solutions, toying with them, and tossing them, in all their complexity, into forms of beauty, instead of piercing on narrowly and in pain after truth absolute and inaccessible. A Wordsworth, he admits, might have a genius of the explorative or mystery-piercing kind, and might come back from his excursions into the region of the metaphysical with handfuls of new truth to be worked up into his phantasies. But even *he* might be too dogmatic; and, as for himself, though he might fancy that occasionally he reached the bourn of the mysterious and caught glimpses beyond, it would be presumption to put his half-seeings into speech for others! If any doubt still remains on this head, the following additional passage from one of his letters will set it at rest :—

"As to the poetical character itself (I mean that sort of which, if I am anything, I am a member) it is not *itself;* it has no self; it is everything and nothing; it has no character; it enjoys light and shade; it lives in gusts; it has as much delight in conceiving an Iago as an Imogen. What shocks the virtuous philosopher delights the chameleon poet. . . . A poet is the most unpoetical thing in existence, because he has no identity; he is continually in, for, and filling, some other body. The sun, the moon, the sea, and men and women who are creatures of impulse, *are* poetical, and have about them an un-

changeable attribute; the poet has none, no identity.
. . . If, then, he has no self, and if I am a poet,
where is the wonder that I should say I would write
no more? Might I not at that very instant have
been cogitating in the character of Saturn and Ops?
It is a wretched thing to confess, but it is a very
fact, that not one word I utter can be taken for
granted as an opinion growing out of my identical
nature. How can it be when I have no nature?
When I am in a room with people, if I am free from
speculating on creations of my own brain, then not
myself goes home to myself, but the identity of every
one in the room begins to press in upon me, so that
I am in a very little time annihilated."

Only on one subject does he profess to have any fixed
opinions—namely, on his own art or craft. " I have
not one opinion," he says, "upon anything except
matters of taste." This is one of the most startling
and significant sayings ever uttered by a man respecting himself.

If I am not mistaken, the definition which Keats
here gives of the poetical character corresponds with
the notion which is most popular. Though critics
distinguish between "subjective" and "objective"
poets, and enumerate men in the one class as famous
as men in the other, yet, in our more vague talk, we
are in the habit of leaving out of view those who are
called "subjective" poets, and seeking the typical poet
among their "objective" brethren, such as Homer and

Shakespeare. How this habit is to be explained— whether it proceeds from a perception that the men of the second order are more truly and purely *poets*, and that the others, though often glorious in poetry, might, in strict science, be referred in half to another genus—I will not inquire. It may be remarked, however, that, be this as it may, it is by no means necessary to go all the length with Keats in the interpretation of his theory, and to fancy that the poet approaching most nearly to the perfect type must be a man having no strong individuality, no permanent moral gesture. Scott, for example, was a man of very distinct character, with a mode of thinking and acting in the society in which he lived as proper to himself as his physiognomy or corporeal figure. So, no doubt, it was with Chaucer and Shakespeare ; and Milton, who may, by much of his poetry, be referred to the same order, was a man with a personality to shake a nation. What is meant is that, when they betook themselves from miscellaneous action among their fellows to the exercise of their art, they all, more or less, allowed their personality to melt and fold itself in the imagination. They all, more or less, at such times, stood within themselves, as within a chamber in which their own hopes, convictions, anxieties, and principles lay about neglected, while they plied their mighty **craft**, like the swing of some gigantic arm, with reference to all without. Keats did the same; only, in his case, the chamber wherein he sat had, by his own confession, very few fixtures or other proper furniture. It was a painter's studio, with very little in it besides the easel.

Still, as cannot be too often repeated, there *are* subtle laws connecting the creations of the most purely artistic poet with his personal character and experience. The imagination, though it seems to fly round and round the personality, and often at a great distance from it, is still attached to it and governed by it in its flight—determined, in its wheelings towards this or that object, by incessant communications from the total mind and reason of which it is at once the efflux, the envoy, and the servitor. Chaucer's poetry would have been different if Chaucer himself had been different; Scott's novels and poems could have been written by no one but a man cast exactly in Scott's mould, even to the bushiness of his eyebrows and the Northumbrian burr of his speech; and, had we the necessary skill in the higher criticism, even the Protean Shakespeare might be chased out of his dramas into his own proper form as he used to walk in the meadows of Stratford-upon-Avon. So also with the poetry of Keats. Impersonal as it is in comparison with such poetry as Shelley's, it has yet a certain assemblage of characteristics, which the reader learns to recognise as distinctive; and these it owes to the character of its author.

At the foundation of the character of Keats lay an extraordinary keenness of all the bodily sensibilities and the mental sensibilities which depend upon them. He led, in great part, a life of passive sensation, of pleasure and pain through the senses. Take a book of Physiology and go over the so-called classes of sensations one by one—the sensations of the mere muscular states; the sensations connected with such vital processes as circulation, alimentation, respiration, and electrical intercommunication with surrounding bodies; the sensations of taste; those of odour; those of touch; those of hearing; and those of sight—and Keats will be found to have been unusually endowed in them all. He had, for example, an extreme sensibility to the pleasures of the palate. The painter Haydon tells a story of his once seeing him cover his tongue with cayenne pepper, in order, as he said, that he might enjoy the delicious sensation of a draught of cold claret after it. " Talking of pleasure," he says himself in one of his letters, " this moment I was writing with one hand, and with the other holding to my mouth a nectarine;" and he goes on to describe the nectarine in language that would re-awaken gustativeness in the oldest fruiterer. This of one of the more ignoble senses, if it is right to call

those senses ignoble that minister the least visibly to
the intellect. But it was the same with the nobler or
more intellectual senses of hearing and sight. He
was passionately fond of music ; and his sensitiveness
to colour, light, and other kinds of visual impression,
was preternaturally acute. He possessed, in short,
simply in virtue of his organization, a rich intellectual foundation of that kind which consists of notions
furnished directly by sensations, and of a corresponding stock of names and terms. Even had he remained
without education, his natural vocabulary of words
for all the varieties of thrills, tastes, odours, sounds,
colours, and tactual perceptions, would have been unusually precise and extensive. As it was, this native
capacity for keen and abundant sensation was developed, educated, and harmonised, by the influences
of reading, intellectual conversation, and more or less
laborious thought, into that richer and more cultivated sensuousness which, under the name of sensibility to natural beauty, is an accepted requisite in
the constitution of painters and poets.

It is a fact on which physiologists have recently
been dwelling much, that the imagination of any
bodily state or action calls into play exactly those
nervous, muscular, and other processes, though in
weaker degree, which are called into play by the real
bodily state or action so simulated. The imagination

of sugar in the mouth causes the same exact flow within the lips which would be caused by sugar really tasted; the imagination of firing a rifle does actually compel to the entire gesture of shooting, down even to the bending of the forefinger round the ideal trigger, though the mimic attitude may be baulked of completion; the imagination of a pain in any part may be persevered in till a pain is actually induced in that part. Whether or not this fact shall ever serve much towards the elucidation of the connexion between the imagination and the personal character—whether or not it may ever be developed into a distinct doctrine that the habits of a man's own real being mark, by an *a priori* necessity, the directions in which his imagination will work most naturally and strongly— one can hardly avoid thinking of it in studying the genius of Keats. The most obvious characteristic of Keats's poetry is certainly its abundant *sensuousness.* Some of his finest little poems are all but literally lyrics of the sensuous, embodiments of the feelings of ennui, fatigue, physical languor, and the like, in tissues of fancied circumstance and sensation. Thus, in the well-known *Ode to the Nightingale*—

> " My heart aches, and a drowsy numbness pains
>   My sense, as though of hemlock I had drunk,
> Or emptied some dull opiate to the drains
>   One minute past, and Lethe-wards had sunk."

In this state he hears the nightingale, and straightway
finds his cure—

" O for a draught of vintage that hath been
  Cool'd a long age in the deep-delvèd earth,
Tasting of Flora and the country-green,
  Dance, and Provençal song, and sunburnt mirth!
O for a beaker full of the warm South,
  Full of the true, the blushful Hippocrene,
    With beaded bubbles winking at the brim
      And purple-stainèd mouth,
    That I might drink, and leave the world unseen,
      And with thee fade away into the forest dim."

It is the same in those longer pieces of narrative phantasy which form the larger portion of his writings.
Selecting, as in *Endymion*, a legend of the Grecian
mythology, or, as in *Isabella, or the Pot of Basil*, a
story from Boccaccio, or, as in *The Eve of St. Agnes*,
the hint of a middle-age superstition, or, as in *Lamia*,
a story of Greek witchcraft, he sets himself to weave
out the little text of substance so given into a linked
succession of imaginary movements and incidents
taking place in the dim depths of ideal scenery,
whether of forest, grotto, sea-shore, the interior of a
Gothic castle, or the marble vestibule of a Corinthian
palace. In following him in these luxurious excursions into a world of ideal nature and life, we see his
imagination winging about, as if it were his disembodied senses hovering insect-like in one humming

group, all keeping together in harmony at the bidding of a higher intellectual power, and yet each catering for itself in that species of circumstance which is its peculiar food. Thus, the disembodied sense of Taste—

> " Here is wine
> Alive with sparkles—never, I aver,
> Since Ariadne was a vintager,
> So cool a purple : taste these juicy pears,
> Sent me by sad Vertumnus, when his fears ⸵
> Were high about Pomona : here is cream
> Deepening to richness from a snowy gleam—
> Sweeter than that nurse Amalthea skimm'd
> For the boy Jupiter ; and here, undimm'd
> By any touch, a bunch of blooming plums
> Ready to melt between an infant's gums."

Or, again, in the description of the dainties in the chapel in the *The Eve of St. Agnes*—

> " And still she slept an azure-lidded sleep
> In blanchèd linen, smooth and lavender'd,
> While he from forth the closet brought a heap
> Of candied apple, quince, and plum, and gourd,
> With jellies soother than the creamy curd,
> And lucent syrups tinct with cinnamon,
> Manna and dates, in argosy transferr'd
> From Fez, and spicèd dainties every one
> From silken Samarcand to cedar'd Lebanon."

As an instance of the disembodied delight in sweet odour, take the lines in *Isabella*—

> " Then in a silken scarf, sweet with the dews
> Of precious flowers pluck'd in Araby,
> And divine liquids come with odorous ooze
> Through the cold serpent-pipe refreshfully,
> She wrapp'd it up."

Delicacy and richness in ideal sensations of touch and sound are found throughout. Thus, even the sensation of cold water on the hands :—

> " When in an antechamber every guest
> Had felt the cold full sponge to pleasure press'd
> By ministering slaves upon his hands and feet " ;

or the ideal tremulation of a string :—

> " Be thou in the van
> Of circumstance ; yea, seize the arrow's barb
> Before the tense string murmur."

But let us pass to the sense of sight, with its various perceptions of colour, light, and lustre. Here Keats is, in some respects, *facile princeps*, even among our most sensuous poets. Here is the description of Lamia while she was still a serpent :—

> " She was a gordian shape of dazzling hue,
> Vermilion-spotted, golden, green, and blue,
> Striped like a zebra, freckled like a pard,
> Eyed like a peacock, and all crimson-barr'd,
> And full of silver moons that, as she breathed,
> Dissolved, or brighter shone, or interwreathed
> Their lustres with the gloomier tapestries."

Here is a passage somewhat more various, the description of the bower in which Adonis was sleeping—

> "Above his head
> Four lily-stalks did their white honours wed
> To make a coronal; and round him grew
> All tendrils green, of every bloom and hue,
> Together intertwined and tramell'd fresh:
> The vine of glossy sprout; the ivy mesh,
> Shading the Ethiop berries; and woodbine,
> Of velvet leaves and bugle-blooms divine;
> Convolvulus in streakèd vases flush;
> The creeper, mellowing for an autumn blush;
> And virgin's bower, trailing airily;
> With others of the sisterhood."

These last quotations suggest a remark which does not seem unimportant. When critics or poets themselves speak of the love of nature or the perception of natural beauty as essential in the constitution of the poet, it will often be found that what they chiefly mean is an unusual sensibility to the pleasures of one of the senses—the sense of sight. What they mean is chiefly a fine sense of form, colour, lustre, and the like. Now, though it may be admitted that, in so far as ministration of material for the intellect is concerned, sight is the most important of the senses, yet this all but absolute identification of love of nature with sensibility to visual pleasures seems

erroneous. It is a kind of treason to the other senses,
all of which are avenues of communication between
nature and the mind, though sight may be the main
avenue. In this respect I believe that one of the
most remarkable characteristics of Keats is the universality of his sensuousness.

But farther. Not only, in popular language, does
the love of nature seem to be identified with a sensibility to the pleasures of the one sense of sight;
but, by a more injurious restriction still, this love of
nature, or perception of natural beauty seems to have
been identified, especially of late, with one class of
the pleasures of this one sense of sight—to wit, the
pleasures derived from the contemplation of vegetation. Roses, lilies, grass, trees, cornfields, ferns, heaths,
and poppies : these are what pass for "nature" with
not a few modern poets and critics of poetry. It
seems as if, since Wordsworth fulminated the advice
to poets to go back to nature and to study nature, it
had been the impression of many that the proper way
to comply with the advice was to walk out in the
fields to some spot where the grass was thick and the
weeds and wild-flowers plentiful, and there lie flat
upon the turf, chins downwards, peering into grasses
and flowers, and inhaling their breath. Now, it ought
to be distinctly represented, in correction of this, that
ever so minute and loving a study of vegetation,

though laudable and delightful in itself, does not
amount to a study of nature—that, in fact, vegetation, though a very respectable part of visible nature,
is not the whole of it.   When night comes, for
example, where or how much is your vegetation
then ? Vegetation is *not* nature : I know no proposition that should be more frequently dinned in
the ears of our young poets than this.   The peculiar
notion of natural beauty involved in the habit spoken
of may be said to have come in with the microscope.
In the ancient Greek poets we have very little of it.
They give us trees and grass and flowers, but they
give them more by mere suggestion; and, so far as
they introduce physical nature at all (which is chiefly
by way of a platform for human action), it is with the
larger forms and aspects of nature that they deal, the
wide and simple modifications of the great natural
elements.   Shakespeare, when he chooses, is minutely
and lusciously rich in his scenes of vegetation (and,
indeed, in comparing modern and romantic with
ancient and classical poets generally, it is clear that,
in this respect, there has been a gradual development
of literary tendency) ; but no man more signally than
Shakespeare keeps the just proportion.   Wordsworth
himself, when he called out for the study of nature,
and set the example in his own case by retiring to the
Lakes, did not commit the error of confounding nature

with vegetation. In that district, indeed, where there are mountains and tarns, incessant cloud-variations, and other forms of nature on the great scale, to employ the eye, it was not likely that it would disproportionately exercise itself on particular banks and gardens or individual herbs and flowers. Such an affection for the minutiæ of vegetation was reserved perhaps for the so-called Cockney poets; and one can see that, if it were once supposed that they introduced the taste, the fact might be humorously explained by recollecting that nature to most of them was nature as seen from Hampstead Heath.

Now, undoubtedly, Keats is great in botanical circumstance. Here is a passage in which he describes the kind of home he would like to live in for the purpose of writing poetry :—

"Ah! surely it must be where'er I find
Some flowery spot, sequester'd, wild, romantic,
That often must have seen a poet frantic;
Where oaks that erst the Druid knew are growing,
And flowers, the glory of one day, are blowing;
Where the dark-leaved laburnum's drooping clusters
Reflect athwart the stream their yellow lustres,
And, intertwined, the cassia's arms unite
With its own drooping buds, but very white;
Where on one side are covert branches hung,
'Mong which the nightingales have always sung
In leafy quiet; where to pry aloof
Between the pillars of the sylvan roof

Would be to find where violet buds are nestling,
And where the bee with cowslip bells was wrestling:
There must be too a ruin dark and gloomy,
To say ' Joy not too much in all that's bloomy.' "

Again, in the hymn to Pan in *Endymion :—*

" O thou whose mighty palace-roof doth hang
From jagged trunks, and overshadoweth
Eternal whispers, glooms, the birth, life, death
Of unseen flowers in heavy peacefulness ;
Who lovest to see the Hamadryads dress
Their ruffled locks where meeting hazels darken,
And through whole solemn hours dost sit and hearken
The dreary melody of bedded reeds
In desolate places where dank moisture breeds
The pipy hemlock to strange overgrowth,
Bethinking thee how melancholy loth
Thou wast to leave fair Syrinx—do thou now,
By thy love's milky brow !
By all the trembling mazes that she ran !
Hear us, great Pan ! "

But, though Keats did " joy in all that is bloomy,"
I do not know that he joyed " too much." Though
luscious vegetation was one of his delights, I do not
think that in him there is such a disproportion between this and other kinds of imagery as there has
been in other and inferior poets. There are sea and
cloud in his poetry, as well as herbage and turf; he
is as rich in mineralogical and zoological circumstance

as in that of botany. His most obvious characteristic,
I repeat, is the universality of his sensuousness. And
this it is, added to his exquisite mastery in language
and verse, that makes it such a luxury to read him.
In reading Shelley, even when we admire him most,
there is always a sense of pain; the influence of
Keats is uniformly soothing. In part, as I have said,
this arises from his exquisite mastery in language and
verse—which, in itself, is one form or result of his
sensuousness. There is hardly any recent poet in connexion with whom the mechanism of verse in relation
to thought may be studied more delightfully. Occasionally, it is true, there is the shock of a horrible
Cockney rhyme. Thus:—

> "I shall again see Phœbus in the morning,
> Or flushed Aurora in the roseate dawning."

Or worse still:—

> "Couldst thou wish for lineage higher
> Than twin-sister of Thalia?"

Throughout, too, there are ungainly traces of the dependence of the matter upon the rhyme. But where,
on the whole, shall we find language softer and
richer, verse more harmonious and sweetly-linked,
and, though usually after the model of some older
poet, more thoroughly novel and original; or where

shall we see more beautifully exemplified the power of that high artifice of rhyme by which, as by little coloured lamps of light thrown out in advance of the prow of their thoughts from moment to moment, poets steer their way so windingly through the fantastic gloom ?

In virtue of that unusual and universal sensuousness which all must discern in Keats (and which, as being perhaps his most distinctive characteristic, I have chosen chiefly to illustrate in the quotations I have made), he would certainly have been very memorable among English poets, even had there been less in him than there was of that power of reflective and constructive intellect by which alone so abundant a wealth of the sensuous could have been ruled and shaped into artistic forms. The earlier poems of Shakespeare were, in the main, tissues of sensuous phantasy; and I believe that, compared even with these, the poems that Keats has left us would not seem inferior, if the comparison could be impartially made. The same might be said of certain portions of Spenser's poetry, the resemblance of which to much of Keats's would strike any reader acquainted with both poets, even if he did not know that Keats was a student of Spenser. Perhaps the likest poet to Keats in the whole list of preceding English poets is William Browne, the author of " Britannia's Pastorals ; " but, rich and pleasant as the poetry of Browne is, beyond much that capricious chance has preserved in greater repute, that of Keats is, in Browne's own qualities of richness and pleasantness, immeasurably superior.

Neither sensuousness alone, however, nor sensuousness governed by a reflective and fanciful intellect, will constitute a great poet. However highly endowed a youthful poet may be in these, his only chance of real greatness is in passing on, by due transition and gradation, to that more matured state of mind in which, though the sensuous may remain and the cool fancy may weave its tissues as before, human interest and sympathy with the human heart and grand human action shall predominate in all. Now, in the case of Keats, there is evidence of the fact of this gradation. There is evidence of a progress both intellectually and morally; of a disposition, already consciously known to himself, to move forward out of the sensuous or merely sensuous-ideal mood, into the mood of the truly epic poet, the poet of life, sublimity and action. Thus, in one of his prose letters, he says, "Although I take Poetry to be the chief, yet there is something else wanting to one who passes his life among books and thoughts of books." And again, "I find earlier days are gone by; I find that I can have no enjoyment in the world but continual drinking of knowledge. I find there is no worthy pursuit but the idea

of doing some good to the world. Some do it with
their society ; some with their art; some with their
benevolence ; some with a sort of power of conferring
pleasure and good humour on all they meet—and, in
a thousand ways, all dutiful to the command of nature.
There is but one way for me. The road lies through
application, study and thought. I will pursue it. I
have been hovering for some time between an exquisite sense of the luxurious and a love for philosophy. Were I calculated for the former, I should be
glad ; but, as I am not, I shall turn all my soul to
the latter." In his poetry we have similar evidence.
Even in his earlier poems one is struck not only by
the steady presence of a keen and subtle intellect, but
also by frequent flashes of permanently deep meaning, frequent lines of lyric thoughtfulness, and occasional maxims of weighty historic generality. What
we have quoted for our special purpose would fail
utterly to convey the proper impression of the merits
of Keats in these respects, or indeed of his poetic
genius generally, unless the memory of the reader
were to suggest the necessary supplement. From *Endymion* itself, sensuous to very wildness as the poem
is considered, scores of passages might be quoted
to prove that already, while it was being written,
intellect, feeling, and experience were doing their work
with Keats—that, to use his own figure, he had

then already advanced for some time out of the Infant Chamber, or Chamber of mere Sensation, into the Chamber of Maiden Thought, and had even there begun to distinguish the openings of the dark passages beyond and around, and to be seized with the longing to explore them. Seeing this, looking then at such of his later poems as *Lamia* and *The Eve of St. Agnes*, and contemplating last of all that wonderful fragment of *Hyperion* which he hurled into the world as he was leaving it, and of which Byron but expressed the common opinion when he said "It seems actually inspired by the Titans, and is as sublime as Æschylus," we can hardly be wrong in believing that, had Keats lived to the ordinary age of man, he would have been one of the greatest of all our poets. As it is, though he died at the age of twenty-five, and left only what in all does not amount to much more than a day's leisurely reading, I believe we shall all be disposed to place him very near indeed to our very best.

V.

THEORIES OF POETRY.

V.

THEORIES OF POETRY.[1]

THERE have been hundreds of disquisitions on poetry in all ages, long and short, good, bad, and indifferent; and, now-a-days, we cannot open a magazine or a review without finding something new said about our friend " *The* Poet," as distinguished from our other friend " *The* Prophet " and the rest. But cant cannot be helped; and, if we are to abandon good phrases because they have been used a great many times, there is an end to all reviewing.

Much, however, as has been spoken about poetry and poets, it may be doubted whether the world, in its meditations on this subject, has got far beyond the antithesis suggested by what Aristotle said about it two thousand years ago, on the one hand, and what Bacon advanced two hundred and fifty years ago, on

[1] *North British Review*, August 1853.—" Poetics: an Essay on Poetry." By E. S. Dallas. London, 1852.

the other. At least, acquainted as we are with a good
deal that Wordsworth, and Coleridge, and Goethe, and
Leigh Hunt, and now Mr. Dallas, have written about
poetry by way of more subtle and insinuating investigation, we still feel that the best notion of the thing,
for any manageable purpose, is to be beaten out of
the rough-hewn definitions of it, from opposite sides,
supplied by Aristotle and Bacon.   In his *Poetics,*
Aristotle writes as follows :—

    " Epic poetry and the poetry of tragedy, as well as
comedy and dithyrambic poetry, and most flute and
lyre music, all are, in their nature, viewed generally,
imitations (μιμήσεις) ; differing from each other, however, in three things—either in that they imitate by
different means, or in that they imitate different things,
or in that they imitate differently and not in the same
manner. For, as some artists, either from technical
training or from mere habit, imitate various objects by
colours and forms, and other artists by vocal sound,
so, of the arts mentioned above, all effect their imitation by rhythm, and words, and melody, employed
either severally or in combination. For example, in
flute and lyre music, and in any other kind of music
having similar effect, such as pipe music, melody and
rhythm are alone used.   In the dance, again, the imitation is accomplished by rhythm by itself, without
melody ; there being dancers who, by means of rhythmical gesticulations, imitate even manners, passions, and
acts.   Lastly, epic poetry produces its imitations either
by mere articulate words, or by metre superadded. . . .

Since, in the second place, those who imitate copy living characters, it behoves imitations either to be of serious and lofty, or of mean and trivial objects. The imitation must, in fact, either be of characters and actions better than they are found among ourselves, or worse, or much the same; just as, among painters, Polygnotus represented people better-looking than they were, Pauson worse-looking, and Dionysius exactly as they were. Now, it is evident that each of the arts above mentioned will have these differences, the difference arising from their imitating different things. In the dance, and in flute and lyre music, these diversities are visible; as also in word-imitations and simple metre. Homer, for example, really made men better than they are; Cleophon made them such as they are; whereas Hegemon, the first writer of parodies, and Nicochares, made them worse. So also, in dithyrambics and lyrics, one might, with Timotheus and Philoxenus, imitate even Persians and Cyclopes. By this very difference, too, is tragedy distinguished from comedy. The one even now strives in its imitations to exhibit men better than they are, the other worse. . . . Still the third difference, remains: namely, as to the manner or form of the imitation. For, even though the means of imitation, and the things imitated, should be the same, there might be this difference, that the imitation might be made either in the form of a narration (and that either through an alien narrator, as Homer does, or in one's own person without changing) or by representing the imitators as all active and taking part. So that, though in one respect Homer and Sophocles would go together as imitators, as both having earnest subjects, in another Sophocles and Aristophanes would

go together, as both imitating dramatically. . . . Two
causes, both of them natural, seem to have operated
together to originate the poetic art. The first is that
the tendency to imitate is innate in men from childhood (the difference between man and other animals
being that he is the most imitative of all, acquiring
even his first lessons in knowledge through imitation)
and that all take pleasure in imitation. . . . . In
the second place, just as the tendency to imitate is
natural to us, so also is the love of melody and of
rhythm ; and metre is evidently a variety of rhythm.
Those, therefore, who from the first were most strongly
inclined to these things by nature, proceeding by little
and little, originated poetry out of their impromptu
fancies. Poetry, thus originated, was broken into departments corresponding to the peculiar characters of
its producers, the more serious imitating only beautiful
actions and their issues, while the more thoughtless
natures imitated mean incidents, inventing lampoons,
as others had invented hymns and eulogies. Before
Homer we have no poem of this kind to be mentioned,
though doubtless many existed."

Such, as indicated in those sentences of the treatise
which seem to be of most essential import, is the
general doctrine of Aristotle as to the nature of Poetry.
With this contrast Bacon's theory, as stated, cursorily
but profoundly, in the following sentences from the
Advancement of Learning :—

" The parts of Human Learning have reference to the
three parts of man's understanding, which is the seat

of learning—History to his Memory; Poesy to his
Imagination; and Philosophy to his Reason. . . . Poesy
is a part of learning, in measure of words for the most
part restrained, but in all other points extremely
licensed, and doth truly refer to the imagination;
which, being not tied to the laws of matter, may at
pleasure join that which Nature hath severed, and
sever that which Nature hath joined, and so make
unlawful matches and divorces of things. *Pictoribus
atque Poetis,* &c. It [Poetry] is taken in two senses—
in respect of words, or matter. In the first sense, it is
but a character of style, and belongeth to the arts of
speech, and is not pertinent for the present; in the
latter, it is, as hath been said, one of the principal
portions of learning, and is nothing else but Feigned
History, which may be styled as well in prose as in
verse. The use of this Feigned History hath been to
give some shadow of satisfaction to the mind of man in
the points wherein the nature of things doth deny it—
the world being in proportion inferior to the soul; by
reason whereof there is agreeable to the spirit of man a
more ample greatness, a more exact goodness, and a
more absolute variety than can be found in the nature
of things. Therefore, because the acts or events of true
history have not that magnitude which satisfieth the
mind of man, Poesy feigneth acts and events greater
and more heroical; because true history propoundeth
the successes and the issues of actions not so agree-
able to the merits of virtue and vice, therefore Poesy
feigneth them more just in retribution, and more
according to revealed Providence; because true history representeth actions and events more ordinary
and less interchanged, therefore Poesy endueth them

with more rareness : so as it appeareth that Poesy
serveth and conferreth to magnanimity, morality, and
delectation. And, therefore, it was ever thought to
have some participation of divineness, because it
doth raise and erect the mind, by submitting the shows
of things to the desires of the mind, whereas Reason
doth buckle and bow the mind unto the nature of
things. . . . In this third part of learning, which is
Poesy, I can report no deficience. For, being as a
plant that cometh of the lust of the earth without a
formal seed, it hath sprung up and spread abroad more
than any other kind."

Now, though it would be possible so to stretch and
comment upon Aristotle's theory of poetry as to make
it correspond with Bacon's, yet, *primâ facie*, the two
theories are different, and even antithetical. If both
are true, it is because the theorists tilt at opposite
sides of the shield. Aristotle makes the essence of
Poetry to consist in its being imitative and truthful ;
Bacon, in its being creative and fantastical. According
to Aristotle, there is a natural tendency in men to the
imitation of what they see in nature ; the various arts
are nothing more than imitations, so to speak, with different kinds of imitating substance ; and poetry is that
art which imitates in articulate language, or, at most,
in language elevated and rendered more rich and exquisite by the addition of metre. According to Bacon,
on the other hand, there is a natural tendency, and

a natural prerogative, in the mind of man to condition the universe anew for its own intellectual satisfaction. It may brood over the sea of actual existences, carrying on the work of creation, with these existences for the material, and its own phantasies and longings for the informing spirit; it may be ever on the wing among nature's sounds and appearances, not merely for the purpose of observing and co-ordinating them, but also that it may delight itself with new ideal combinations, severing what nature has joined, and joining what nature has put asunder. Poetry, in accordance with this view, might perhaps be defined as the art of producing, by means of articulate language, metrical or unmetrical, a *fictitious concrete*, either like to something existing in nature, or, if unlike anything there existing, justifying that unlikeness by the charm of its own impressiveness.

Amid all the discussions of all the critics as to the nature of poetry, this antagonism, if such it is, between the Aristotelian and the Baconian theories, will be found eternally reproducing itself.

When Wordsworth defined poetry to be " emotion recollected in tranquillity," and declared it to be the business of the poet to represent out of real life, and as nearly as possible in the language of real life, scenes and events of an affecting or exciting character, he reverted, and with good effect, to the imitation-theory of Aristotle. All Coleridge's disquisitions, on the other hand, even when his friend Wordsworth is the theme and exemplar, are subtle developments of the imagination-theory of Bacon. His famous remark that the true antithesis is not Poetry and Prose, but Poetry and Science, is but another form of Bacon's remark, that, whereas it is the part of Reason " to buckle and bow the mind to the nature of things," it is the part of Imagination, as the poetical faculty, " to raise the mind by submitting the shows of things to its desires." And so with the definitions, more or less formal, of other writers. Thus Leigh Hunt: " Poetry is the utterance of a passion for truth, beauty, and power, embodying and illustrating its conceptions by imagination and fancy, and modulating its language on the principle of variety in uniformity." That this definition, notwithstanding that it is constructed on the principle of omitting nothing that any one would like to see included, is yet essentially a glimpse from the Baconian side of the shield, is obvious from the fact that its author afterwards uses as synonymous with it the abbreviations " Imaginative passion," " Passion for imaginative pleasure." Lastly, Mr. Dallas, with all his ingenuity, does not really get much farther in the end. Beginning with an expression of dissatisfaction with all existing definitions of poetry, Aristotle's and Bacon's included, as being definitions of the thing not in itself, but in its accidents, he proceeds first, very properly, to make a distinction between poetical feeling, which all men have, and the art of poetical expression, which is the prerogative of those who are called poets. Both are usually included under the term Poetry; but, to avoid confusion, Mr. Dallas proposes to use the general term Poetry for the poetical feeling, and to call the art which caters for that feeling Poesy. Then, taking for his guide the fact that all have agreed that, whatever poetry is, it has *pleasure* for its end, he seeks to work his way to the required definition through a prior analysis of the nature of pleasure. Having, as the result of this analysis, defined pleasure to be "the harmonious and unconscious activity of the soul," he finds his way then clear. For there are various kinds of pleasure, and poetry is one of these. It is "imaginative pleasure;" or, if we write the thing more fully out, it is the "imaginative harmonious and unconscious activity of the soul," or that kind of harmonious and unconscious activity of the soul which consists in the exercise of the imagination. Poesy, of course, is the corresponding art, the art of producing what will give imaginative pleasure. Now, with all our respect for the ability with which Mr. Dallas conducts his investigation, and our relish for the many lucid and deep remarks which drop from his pen in the course of it, we must say that, as respects the main matter in discussion, his investigation does not leave us fully satisfied. "Poetry is imaginative pleasure": very well; but Bacon had said substantially the same thing when he described poetry as a kind of literature having reference to the imagination; and Leigh Hunt had, as we have seen, anticipated the exact phrase, defining poetry to be "imaginative passion," and the faculty of the poet to be the faculty of "producing imaginative pleasure." In short, the whole difficulty, the very essence of the question, consists not in the word *pleasure,* but in the word *imaginative.* Had Mr. Dallas bestowed half the pains on the illustration of what is meant by imagination that he has bestowed on the analysis of what is meant by pleasure, he would have done the science of poetry more service. This— the nature of the imaginative faculty—is "the vaporous drop profound that hangs upon the corner of the moon," and Mr. Dallas has not endeavoured to catch it. His chapter upon the Law of Imagination is one of the most cursory in the book; and the total result, as far as a fit definition of poetry is concerned, is that he ends in finding himself in the same hut with Bacon, after having refused its shelter.

The antagonism between the Aristotelian theory, which makes poetry to consist in imitative passion, and the Baconian theory, which makes it to consist in imaginative passion, is curiously reproducing itself at present [1853] in the kindred art of painting. Pre-Raphaelitism is in painting very much what the reform led by Wordsworth was in poetical literature. Imitate nature; reproduce her exact and literal forms; do not paint ideal trees or vague recollections of trees, ideal brick-walls or vague recollections of brick-walls, but actual trees and actual brick-walls; dismiss from your minds the trash of Sir Joshua Reynolds about "correcting nature," "improving nature," and the like;—such are the maxims addressed by the Pre-Raphaelites, both with brush and with pen, to their fellow-artists. All this is, we say, a return to the theory of Aristotle, which makes the essence of art to consist in Imitation, and a protest against that of Bacon, which makes the essence of art to consist in Ideali-zation. Poor Sir Joshua Reynolds ought to fall back upon Bacon, so that, when he is next attacked for his phrases "improving nature" and the like, the Pre-Raphaelites may see looming behind him the more formidable figure of a man whose words no one dares to call trash, and whose very definition of art was couched in expressions like these: "There is, agree-able to the spirit of man, a more ample greatness, a more exact goodness, and a more absolute variety than can be found in the nature of things " "The use of feigned history is to give to the mind of man some shadow of satisfaction in those points wherein the

nature of things doth deny it." The battle, we say,
must be fought with these phrases. Nor is the battle
confined to the art of painting. There is a more
restricted kind of Pre-Raphaelitism now making its
way in the department of fictitious literature. Admiring the reality, the truthfulness, of Thackeray's delineations of life and society, there are men who will
have nothing to do with what they call the phantasies and caricatures of the Dickens school. The
business of the novelist, they say, is to represent men
as they are, with all their foibles as well as their
virtues; in other words, to imitate real life. Here
again comes in the Baconian thunder. " Because the
acts or events of true history have not that magnitude
which satisfieth the mind of man, poesy (and Bacon's
definition of poesy includes prose fiction) feigneth
acts and events greater and more heroical." Whether
Dickens can take the benefit of this authority, in
those cases where he is charged with unreality, we
need not inquire; it evidently points, however, to a
possible style of prose fiction different from that of
Fielding and Thackeray, and yet as legitimate in the
view of art.

For ourselves, we hold the imitation-theory as
applied to poetry or art to be so inadequate in
essential respects that it would be time lost to try
to mend it; and we find no suitable statement of

what seems to be the very idea of poetry, except in some definition like that of Bacon.

Only consider the matter for a moment. Take any piece of verse from any poet, and in what single respect can that piece of verse be said to be an imitation of nature? In the first place, that it is verse at all is a huge deviation in itself from what is, in any ordinary sense, natural. Men do not talk in good literary prose, much less in blank verse or rhyme. Macbeth, in his utmost strait and horror—Lear, when the lightnings scathed his white head—did not actually talk in metre. Even Bruce at Bannockburn did not address his army in trochees. Here, then, at the very outset, there is a break-down in the theory of Imitation, or literal truth to nature. And all prose literature shares in this break-down. Not a single personage in Scott's novels would have spoken precisely as Scott makes them speak; nay, nor is there a single character in Thackeray himself strictly and in every respect a fac-simile of what is real. Correct grammar, sentences of varied lengths and of various cadences, much more octosyllabic or pentameter verse, and still more rhymed stanzas, are all artificialities. Literature has them, but in real life they are not to be found. It is as truly a deviation from nature to represent a king talking in blank verse, or a lover plaining in rhyme, as it is, in an opera, to make a martyr sing a song and be encored before being thrown into the flames. So far as truth to nature is concerned, an opera, or even a ballet, is hardly more artificial than a drama. Suppose, however, that, in order to escape from this difficulty, it should be said that metre, rhyme, rhetorical consecutiveness, and the like, are conditions previously and for other reasons existing in the material in which the imitation is to take place: would the theory of imitation or truth to nature even then hold good? Let it be granted that grammatical and rhythmical prose is a kind of marble, that blank verse is a kind of jasper, and that rhymed verse is a kind of amethyst or opaline; that the selection of those substances as the materials in which the imitation is to be effected is a thing already and independently determined on; and that it is only in so far as imitation can be achieved consistently with the nature of those substances that imitation and art are held to be synonymous. Will the theory even then look the facts in the face? It will not. In the time of Aristotle, indeed, when most Greek poetry was, to a greater degree than poetry is now, either directly descriptive or directly narrative, the theory might have seemed less astray than it must to us. Even then, however, it was necessarily at fault. The Achilles and the Ajax of Homer, the Œdipus and the Antigone of Sophocles, were, in no sense, imitations from nature; they were ideal beings, never seen on any Ægæan coast, and dwelling nowhere save in the halls of imagination. Aristotle himself felt this; and hence, at the risk of cracking into pieces his own fundamental theory, he indulges occasionally in a strain like that of Bacon when he maintains that poetry "representeth actions and events less ordinary and interchanged, and endueth them with more rareness," than is found in nature. "The poet's business," says Aristotle, "is not to tell events as they have actually happened, but as they possibly might happen." And again: "Poetry is more philosophical and more sublime than history." Very true: but what then becomes of the imitation? In what possible sense can there be imitation unless there is something to be imitated? If that something is ideal, if it exists not actually and outwardly, but only in the mind of the artist, then imitation is the wrong word to use.

All this will be much more obvious if we refer to modern poetry. Here is a stanza from Spenser—part of his description of the access to Mammon's cave He has just described Revenge, Jealousy, Fear, Shame and other entities.

> " And over them sad Horror with grim hue
>   Did always soar, beating his iron wings;
>   And after him owls and night-ravens flew,
>   The hateful messengers of heavy things,
>   Of death and dolour telling sad tidings

P

> While sad Celeno, sitting on a clift,
> A song of bale and bitter sorrow sings,
> That heart of flint asunder could have rift ;
> Which having ended, after him she flieth swift."

This is true poetry; and yet, by no possible ingenuity, short of that which identified King Jeremiah with pickled cucumbers, could it be shown to consist of imitation. If it be said that it is mimic creation, and that this is the sense in which Aristotle meant his imitation, or μίμησις, to be understood, we shall be very glad to accept the explanation; but then we shall have to reply that, as the essence of the business lies in the word " creation " as the substantive of the phrase, it is a pity the brunt of the disquisition should have been borne so long by the adjective. Aristotle, we believe, did mean that poetry was, in the main, fiction, or invention of fables in imitation of nature; but, unfortunately, even then he misleads by making imitation, which is but the jackal in the treatise, seem the lion in the definition. Nor even then will his theory be faultless and complete. Spenser's grim-hued Horror, soaring aloft, beating his iron wings, and with owls and night-ravens after him, is certainly a creation; but in what sense it is a *mimic* creation, or a creation in imitation of nature, it would take a critic, lost to all reasonable use of words, to show.

In short, and to close this discussion with a phrase

which seems to us to fall like a block of stone through all our reasonings about art imitating nature, being true to nature, and the like, "Art is *called* art," said Goethe, "simply because it is *not* nature." This, it will be seen, is identical with Bacon's poesy "submitting the shows of things to the desires of the mind." Only in one sense can it be said that the art itself comes under the denomination of nature. Thus, Shakespeare—

> "E'en that art,
> Which, you say, adds to nature, is an art
> That nature makes."

True, as Goethe would have been the first to admit! In this sense, Spenser's grim-hued Horror beating his iron wings *was* a part of nature, because, in this sense, the poet's own soul, with that very imagination starting out of it, was involved and contained in the universal round. But in any sense in which the words art and nature are available for the purposes of critical exposition, Goethe's saying is irrefragable: "Art is *called* art simply because it is *not* nature." Dissolve the poet through nature, regard the creative act itself as a part of nature, and then, of course, poetry or art is truth to nature. But keep them distinct, as you must do if you talk of imitation, and then the poet is nature's master, changer, tyrant, lover, watcher, slave, and mimic, all in one, his head now low in her lap and again, a moment after, she scared **and** weeping because, though he is with her, he **minds** her not.

All this, we believe, it is very necessary to say. Pre-Raphaelitism in painting, like Wordsworth's reform in poetical literature (which reform consisted in the precept and example of what may be called Pre-Drydenism), we regard, so far as it is a recall of art to truth and observation, as an unmixed good. But it is essentially, in this particular respect, a reform only in the *language* of art; and art itself is not language, but the creative use of it. We believe the Pre-Raphaelites know this ; for, though, in theorizing, they naturally put forward their favourite idea of imitation or truthfulness, yet in their practice they are as much imaginative artists as imitative. While in any of the higher Pre-Raphaelite paintings the *language* of the painting—that is, the flowers, grasses, foliage, brick-walls, and costumes—may be more real and true to fact than elsewhere, yet the *thought* which this language is used to convey is as ideal, as much a supposition, imagination, or recombination, as much a mere wish or *utinam*, as in the majority of other pictures. Still, in our theory of art at the present day, or at least in our theory of literary art, the notion of imitation is beginning to exist in excess. The very power of that most admirable novelist, Thackeray, is beginning to spoil us.

We will have nothing but reality, nothing but true
renderings of men and women as they are ; no giants or
demigods any more, but persons of ordinary stature,
and the black and the white in character so mixed that
people shall neither seem crows nor white doves, but
all more or less magpies. Good, certainly, all this ;
but, had the rule always been peremptory, where had
been our Achilleses, our Prometheuses, our Tancreds,
our Lears, our Hamlets, our Fausts, our Egmonts ;
these men that never were, these idealizations of what
might be—not copied from nature, but imagined and
full-fashioned by the soul of man, and thence disen-
chained into nature, magnificent phantasms, to roam
amid its vacancies ? Nor will it do to exempt the epic
and the tragic muses, and to subject to the rule only
the muse of prose fiction. Where, in that case, had
been our Quixotes, our Pantagruels and Panurges, our
Ivanhoes and Rebeccas, our Fixleins and Siebenkaeses ?
These were sublimations of nature, not imitations ;
suggestions to history by genius and an inspired philosophy. The muse of prose literature is very hardly
dealt with. Why in prose may there not be much of
that license in the fantastic, that measured riot, that
right of whimsy, that unabashed dalliance with the
extreme and beautiful, which the world allows by prescription to verse ? Why may not prose chase forest-
nymphs, and see little green-eyed elves, and delight in

peonies and musk-roses, and invoke the stars, and roll
mists about the hills, and watch the seas thundering
through caverns and dashing against promontories ?
Why, in prose, quail from the grand or ghastly on the
one hand, or blush with shame at too much of the
exquisite on the other? Is prose made of iron ? Must
it never weep, never laugh, never linger to look at a
buttercup, never ride at a gallop over the downs ?
Always at a steady trot, transacting only such business
as may be done within the limits of a soft sigh on the
one hand and a thin smile on the other, must it leave
all finer and higher work of imagination to the care
of Verse ? Partly so, perhaps ; for prose soon becomes
ashamed, and, when highly inspired, lifts itself into
metre. Yet it is well for literature that there should
be among us such prose-poets as Richter was to the
Germans : men avoiding nothing as too fantastic for
their element, but free and daring in it as the verse-
poet in his. All honour to Thackeray and the prose-
fiction of social reality ; but let us not so theorize as to
exclude from prose-fiction the boundless imagination of
another Richter, or even the lawless zanyism of another
Rabelais.

Poetry, then, we must, after all, define in terms
tantamount to those of Bacon. With Bacon himself
we may define it vaguely as having reference to the

imagination, " which faculty submitteth the shows of
things to the desires of the mind, whereas reason doth
buckle and bow the mind unto the nature of things."
Or we may vary the phrase, and, with Coleridge, call it
" the vision and faculty divine ; " or, with Leigh Hunt,
" imaginative passion," the passion for " imaginative
pleasure ; " or, with Mr. Dallas, more analytically, " the
imaginative, harmonious, and unconscious activity of
the soul." In any case, IMAGINATION is the main word,
the main idea. Upon this Shakespeare himself has put
his seal :

> " The lunatic, the lover, and the poet,
> Are of *imagination* all compact."

In short, poesy is what the Greek language recognised
it to be—ποίησις, or creation. The antithesis, therefore, *is* between Poetry and Science—ποίησις and
νόησις. Let the universe of all accumulated existence, inner and outer, material and mental, up to the
present moment, lie under one like a sea, and there
are two ways in which it may be intellectually dealt
with and brooded over. On the one hand, the intellect of man may brood over it inquiringly, striving to
penetrate it through and through, to understand the
system of laws by which its multitudinous atoms are
held together, to master the mystery of its pulsations
and sequences. This is the mood of the man of
science. On the other hand, the man of intellect may

brood over it creatively, careless how it is held together, or whether it is held together at all, and regarding it only as material to be submitted farther to the operation of a combining energy, and lashed and beaten up into new existences. This is the mood of the poet. The poet is emphatically the man who continues the work of creation; who forms, fashions, combines, imagines; who breathes his own spirit into things; who conditions the universe anew according to his whim and pleasure; who bestows heads of brass on men when he likes, and sees beautiful women with arms of azure; who walks amid Nature's appearances, divorcing them, rematching them, interweaving them, starting at every step flocks of white-winged phantasies that fly and flutter into the ether of the future.

All very well; but, in plain English, what is meant by this imagination, this creative faculty, which is allowed by all to be the characteristic of the poet? Mr. Dallas tells us that psychologists differ in their definitions of imagination. Dugald Stewart, and others, he says, have regarded it solely as the faculty which looks to the possible and unknown, which invents hippogriffs and the like ideal beasts—in short, the creative faculty proper. Mr. Dallas maintains that this is not sufficient, and that the faculty unphilosophically called Conception, the faculty which mirrors or reproduces the real, must also be included in the poetic imagination. And this is nearly all that he says on the subject.

Now, if we were to venture on a closer definition, such as might be found applicable over the whole domain of poetry, we should perhaps affirm something to the following effect :—The poetic or imaginative faculty is *the power of intellectually producing a new or artificial concrete ;* and the poetic genius or temperament is *that disposition of mind which leads habitually, or by preference, to this kind of intellectual exercise.*

There is much in this statement that might need explanation. In the first place, we would call attention to the words " intellectually producing," " intellectual exercise." These words are not needlessly inserted. It seems to us that the distinct recognition of what is implied in them would save a great deal of confusion. The phrases " poetic fire," " poetic passion," and the like, true and useful as they are on proper occasion, are calculated sometimes to mislead. There may be fire, there may be passion in the poet ; but that which is peculiar to the poet, that which constitutes the poetic tendency as such, is a special *intellectual* habit, distinct from the intellectual habit of the man of science. The poetic process may be set in operation by, and accompanied by, any amount of passion or feeling; but the poetic process itself, so far as distinctions are of any value, is an *intellectual* process. Farther, as to its

kind, it is the intellectual process of producing a new
or artificial concrete.   This distinguishes poetry at once,
in all its varieties, and whether in verse or in prose,
from the other forms of literature.   In scientific or
expository literature the tendency is to the abstract,
to the translation of the facts and appearances of
nature into general intellectual conceptions and forms
of language.   In oratorical literature, or the literature
of moral stimulation, the aim is to urge the mind in
a certain direction, or to induce upon it a certain state.
There remains, distinct from either of these, the literature of the concrete, the aim of which is to represent
the facts and appearances of nature and life, or to form
out of them new concrete combinations.   There are men
who delight in things simply because they have happened, or because they can imagine them to happen:
men, for example, to whom it is a real pleasure to
know that at such and such a time a knight in armour
rode along that way and across that bridge; who dwell
with relish on such a fact as that Sulla had a face
mottled white and red, so that an Athenian wit compared it to a mulberry dipped in meal; who can go
back to that moment, and re-arrest time there, as in a
picture, when Manlius hung half-way from the top of
the Tarpeian rock, and had his death of blood yet
beneath him, or when Marie Antoinette lay under the
axe and it had not fallen; to whom also the mere em-

bodiments of their own fancy or of the fancy of others
are visions they never tire to gaze on. These are the
votaries of the concrete. Now, so far as that literature of
the concrete whose business it is to gratify such feelings
deals merely with the actual facts of the past as delivered
to it by memory, it resolves itself into the department
of *History;* but, so far as it remains unexhausted by
such a subduction, it is *Poetry* or *Creative Literature.*
In practice, as we all know, the two shade into each
other, the historian often requiring and displaying the
imagination of the poet, and the poet, on the other hand,
often relapsing into the describer and the historian.
And here a part of our definition may be found fault
with. Inasmuch as the poet does not necessarily, in
every case, invent scenes and incidents totally ideal,
but often treats poetically the actual fields and landscapes of the earth and the real incidents of life—
so that, in fact, much of our best and most genuine
poetry is descriptive and historical—why define poesy
to be the production of a new or artificial concrete?
Why not call it either the reproduction of an old or
the production of a new concrete? The objection is
that the division which would be thus established is
not fundamental. In every piece of poetry, even the
most descriptive and historical, that which makes it
poetical is not the concrete as furnished by sheer recollection, but the concrete as shaped and bodied forth

anew by the poet's thought—that is, as factitious and
artificial. Shelley, indeed, very sweetly calls poetry
"the record of the best and happiest moments of the
best and happiest minds;" but then this only refers
us farther back in time for the poetry, which certainly
does not consist in the act of recording, if it *be* only
recording, but already lay in the good and happy
moments that are recorded. Thus, if it be said that the
beautiful passage in Wordsworth describing a winter
landscape, with the lake on which he skated with his
companions in his boyhood, is a mere transcript of a
scene from recollection, it may be replied that, if this
is the case (which we do not admit), then the poetry of
the passage was transacted along with the skating, and
the critic, instead of watching the man at his writing-
table, must keep by the side of the boy on the ice. In
short, in every case whatever, poetry is the production
of an artificial concrete—artificial either in *toto*, or in
so far as it is matter of sense or memory worked
into form by the infusion of a meaning. The word
"artificial" has bad associations connected with it;
but, as Hazlitt said of Allegory, it is really a harmless
word, and "won't bite you." It is only necessary to
see what it means here to like it well enough.

The poetical tendency, then, is the tendency to that
kind of mental activity which consists in the production (one might almost say secretion) by the mind of

an artificial concrete; and the poetic genius is that
kind or condition of mind to which this kind of
activity is constitutionally most delightful and easy.
Of the legitimacy of such a mode of activity what
need to say anything? With some theorists, indeed,
poets are little better than privileged liars, and poetry
is little better than the art of lying so as to give pleasure. Even Bacon, with his synonyms of "feigned
history" and the like, evidently means to insinuate a
kind of contempt for poetry as compared with philosophy. The one he calls "the theatre," where it is not
good to stay long; the other is the "judicial place or
palace of the mind." This is natural enough in a man
the tenor of whose own intellectual work must have
inclined him, apart even from the original constitutional bias which determined *that*, to prefer the
exercise which "buckled and bowed the mind to the
nature of things" to the exercise which "elevates
the mind by submitting the shows of things to its
desires." But recognising, as he did, that the one
exercise is, equally with the other, the exercise of a
faculty which is part and parcel of the human constitution, he was not the man to go very far with the
joke about poets being a species of liars. That, we
believe, was Bentham's fun. One can see what a good
thing might be made of it. "Why was that poor
fellow transported? Why, the fact is, at last assizes,

he originated a piece of new concrete, which the law
calls perjury." But the joke may be taken by the other
end. When that deity of the Grecian mythology (if the
Grecian mythology had such a deity) whose function
it was to create trees, walked one sultry day over the
yet treeless earth, and when, chancing to lie down
in a green spot, the creative phrenzy came upon him,
his thought rushed forth, and, with a whirr of earthy
atoms all round and a tearing of turf, the first of oaks
sprang up completed, that also was the origination of
a new piece of concrete, but one could hardly say that
it was telling a lie. Had his godship been a philosopher instead of a poet, had he buckled and bowed
his mind to the nature of things instead of accom-
modating the shows of things to his desires, the world
might have been without oaks to this very day.

Poetical activity being defined generally to be that
kind of intellectual activity which results in the production of new matter of the concrete, it follows that
there are as many varieties in the exercise of this
activity as there are possible forms of an intellectual
concrete. To attempt a complete enumeration of the
various ways in which imaginative activity may show
itself would be tedious; but an instance or two may
bring some of the more common of them before the
mind.

" The sun had just sunk below the tops of the mountains, whose long shadows stretched athwart the valley;
but his sloping rays, shooting through an opening of
the cliffs, touched with a yellow gleam the summits of
the forest that hung upon the opposite steeps, and
streamed in full splendour upon the towers and battlements of a castle that spread its extensive ramparts
along the brow of a precipice above. The splendour
of these illuminated objects was heightened by the contrasted shade which involved the valley below."

Mrs. Radcliffe.

" Almost at the root
Of that tall pine, the shadow of whose bare
And slender stem, while here I sit at eve,
Oft stretches towards me, like a long straight path,
Traced faintly on the greensward—there, beneath
A plain blue stone, a gentle dalesman lies."

Wordsworth.

These are plain instances of that kind of imaginative
exercise which consists in the imagination of *scenes* or
objects. A large proportion of the imaginative activity
of men generally, and of authors in particular, is of
this kind. It includes pictures and descriptions of all
varieties, from the most literal reproductions· of the
real, whether in country or town, to the most absolute
phantasies in form and colour, and from the scale of a
single object, such as the moon or a bank of violets,
to the scale of a Wordsworthian landscape, or of a
Milton's universe with its orbs and interspaces. It
may be called descriptive imagination.

" And Priam then alighted from his chariot,
  Leaving Idæus with it, who remained
  Holding the mules and horses; and the old man
  Went straight in-doors, where the beloved of Jove,
  Achilles sat, and found him.   In the room
  Were others, but apart; and two alone—
  The hero Automedon and Alcinous,
  A branch of Mars—stood by him.   They had been
. At meals, and had not yet removed the board.
  Great Priam came, without their seeing him,
  And, kneeling down, he clasped Achilles' knees,
  And kissed those terrible homicidal hands
  Which had deprived him of so many sons."

HOMER.

This is the imagination of *incident,* or narrative imagination.   The instance is plain even to baldness; it is
direct Homeric narration: but for this very reason it
will better stand as a type of that department of
imaginative activity to which it belongs.   In this
department are included all narrations of incidents,
whether historical and real, or fictitious and supernatural, from the scale of a single incident as told
in a ballad, up to the sustained unity of the epos or
drama, as in *Crusoe, Don Quixote,* the *Iliad,* the *Divine
Comedy,* the *Faery Queene, Macbeth,* or *Paradise Lost.*
It is hardly necessary to point out that the narration
of incident always involves a certain amount of description of scenery.

" The Reve was a slender colerike man,
　His beard was a shave as nigh as ever he can,
　His hair was by his eares round yshorn,
　His top was docked like a priest beforne.
　Full longe were his legges and full lean,
　Ylike a staff ; there was no calf yseen."

CHAUCER.

This may stand as a specimen of what is in reality a sub-variety of the imaginative exercise first mentioned, but is important enough to be adverted to apart. It may be called the imagination of *physiognomy* and *costume ;* under which head might be collected an immense number of passages from all quarters of our literature. This department, too, will include both the real and ideal—the real, as in Chaucer's and Scott's portraits of men and women ; the ideal, as in Spenser's personifications, in Ariosto's hippogriff, or in Dante's Nimrod in a pit in hell, with his face as large as the dome of St. Peter's, and his body in proportion, blowing a horn, and yelling gibberish.

　Connected with this in practice, but distinguishable from it, is another variety of imaginative exercise, which may be called the imagination of *states of feeling.* Here is an example :—

" A fig for those by law protected !
　Liberty 's a glorious feast ;
　Courts for cowards were erected ;
　Churches built to please the priest."

BURNS's *Jolly Beggars.*

This stanza, it will be observed (and we have chosen it on purpose), is, in itself, as little poetical as may be; it is mere harsh Chartist prose.   But, in so far as it is an imagined piece of concrete—that is, in so far as it is an imagination by the poet of the state of feeling of another mind, or of his own mind in certain circumstances—it is poetical.   This is an important consideration, for it links the poet not only with what is poetical in itself, but with a whole, much larger, world of what is unpoetical in itself.   The poet may imagine opinions, doctrines, heresies, cogitations, debates, expositions; there is no limit to his traffic with the moral any more than with the sensuous appearances of the universe : only, as a poet, he deals with all these as concrete things, existing in the objective air, and from which his own mind stands disentangled, as a spade stands loose from the sand it digs, whether sand of gold or sand of silex.   The moment any of the doctrines he is dealing with melts into his own personal state of being (which is happening continually), at that moment the poet ceases to be a poet pure, and becomes so far a thinker or moralist in union with the poet.   As regards the literary range of this kind of imaginative exercise,—the imagination of states of feeling,—it is only necessary to remember what a large proportion it includes of our lyric poetry, and how far it extends into the epic and the drama, where (and especially in the drama) it forms, together with the imagination of physiognomy and costume, the greater part of what is called invention of *character*.

The foregoing is but a slight enumeration of some of the various modes of imaginative exercise as they are popularly distinguishable; and, in transferring them into creative literature at large, they must be conceived as incessantly interblended, and as existing in all varieties and degrees of association with personal thought, personal purpose, and personal calm or storm of feeling. It is matter of common observation, however, that some writers excel more in one and some more in another of the kinds of imagination enumerated. One writer is said to excel in descriptions, but to be deficient in plot and incident; nay, to excel in that kind of description which consists in the imagination of form, but to be deficient in that which consists in the imagination of colour. Another is said to excel in plot, but to be poor in the invention of character, and in other particulars. In short, the imagination, though in one sense it acts loose and apart from the personality, flying freely round and round it, like a sea-bird round a rock, seems, in a deeper sense, restricted by the same law as the personality in its choice and apprehension of the concrete. The organ of ideality, as the phrenologist would say, is the organ by which man freely bodies forth an ideal objective; and yet, were

ideality never so large in a man's head, it would be of
no use to apply it, after Keats or Milton, in the direction of white pinks, pansies freaked with jet, sapphire
battlements, and crimson-lipped shells, unless there
were also a little knot on the eyebrow over the organ
of colour.

The poetical tendency of the human mind being this
tendency to the ideal concrete, to the imagination of
scenes, incidents, physiognomies, states of feeling, and
so on—and all men having more or less of this tendency, catering for them in the ideal concrete, very
much in the same way as their senses cater for them
in the real (so that the imagination of a man might
be said to be nothing more than the ghosts of his
senses wandering in an unseen world)—it follows that
the poet, *par excellence,* is simply the man whose intellectual activity is consumed in this kind of exercise.
All men have imagination; but the poet is " of imagination all compact." He lives and moves in the ideal
concrete.   He teems with imaginations of forms,
colours, incidents, physiognomies, feelings, and characters.   The ghosts of his senses are as busy in an
unseen world of sky, sea, vegetation, cities, highways,
thronged markets of men, and mysterious beings belonging even to the horizon of *that* existence, as his
real senses are with all the nearer world of nature and

life. But the notable peculiarity lies in this, that every thought of his in the interest of *this* world is an excursion into *that*. In this respect, the theory which has been applied to the exposition of the Grecian mythology applies equally to poetic genius in general. The essence of the mythical process, it is said, lay in this, that, the earlier children of the earth having no abstract language, every thought of theirs, of whatever kind, and about whatever matter, was necessarily a new act of imagination, a new excursion in the ideal concrete. If they thought of the wind, they did not think of a fluid rushing about, but of a deity blowing from a cave; if they thought of virtue rewarded, they saw the idea in the shape of a visible transaction, in some lone place, between beings human and divine. And so with the poetical mode of thought to this day. Every thought of the poet, about whatever subject, is transacted not mainly in propositional language, but for the most part in a kind of phantasmagoric or representative language, of imaginary scenes, objects, incidents, and circumstances. To clothe his feelings with *circumstance;* to weave forth whatever arises in his mind into an objective tissue of imagery and incident that shall substantiate it and make it visible: such is the constant aim and art of the poet. Take an example. The idea of life occurs to the poet Keats, and how does he express it?

" Stop and consider !   Life is but a day ;
   A fragile dew-drop on its perilous way
   From a tree's summit ; a poor Indian's sleep,
   While his boat hastens to the monstrous steep
   Of Montmorenci.   Why so sad a moan ?
   Life is the rose's hope while yet unblown ;
   The reading of an ever-changing tale ;
   The light uplifting of a maiden's veil ;
   A pigeon tumbling in clear summer air ;
   A laughing school-boy, without grief or care,
   Riding the springy branches of an elm."

This is true ποίησις.   What with the power of innate analogy, what with the occult suasion of the rhyme, there arose first in the poet's mind, contemporaneous with the idea of life, nay, as incorporate with that idea, the imaginary object or vision of the dew-drop falling through foliage.   That imagined circumstance is, therefore, flung forth as representative of the idea. But even this does not exhaust the creative force.   The idea bodies itself again in the new imaginary circumstance of the Indian in his boat ; and that, too, is flung forth.   Then there is a rest.   But the idea still buds, still seeks to express itself in new circumstance ; and five other translations of it follow.   And these seven pictures, these seven morsels of imagined concrete, if we suppose them all to be intellectually genuine, are as truly the poet's *thoughts* about life as any seven scientific definitions would be the thoughts of the physiologist or the metaphysician. And so in other instances. Tennyson's *Vision of Sin* is a continued phantasmagory of scene and incident representative of a meaning; and, if the meaning is not plain throughout, it is because it would be impossible for the poet himself to translate every portion of it out of that language of phantasmagory in which alone it came into existence. Again, Spenser's personifications—his grim-hued Horror soaring on iron wings, his Jealousy seated apart and biting his lips, and the rest—are all thoughts expressed in circumstance, the circumstance in this case being that of costume and physiognomy. In short, every thought of the poet is an imagination of concrete circumstance of some kind or other—circumstance of visual scenery, of incident, of physiognomy, of feeling, or of character. The poet's thought, let the subject be what it may, brings him to

" Visions of all places : a bowery nook
  Will be elysium—an eternal book
  Whence he may copy many a lovely saying
  About the leaves and flowers—about the playing
  Of nymphs in woods and fountains, and the shade
  Keeping a silence round a sleeping maid ;
  And many a verse from so strange influence
  That we must ever wonder how and whence
  It came."

Regarding the poet, then, considered in his nature, we may sum up by saying that the act of cogitation with him is nothing else than the *intellectual secretion of fictitious circumstance*—the nature of the circumstance in each case depending on the operation of those mysterious affinities which relate thought to the world of sense. In regarding the poet more expressly as a literary artist, all that we have to do is to vary the phrase, and say—the intellectual *invention* of fictitious circumstance. This will apply to all that is truly poetical in literature, whether on the large scale or on the small. In every case what is poetical in literature consists of the embodiment of some notion or feeling, or some aggregate of notions and feelings, in appropriate imagined circumstances. Thus, in historical or biographical writing, the poetic faculty is shown by the skill, sometimes conscious and sometimes unconscious, with which the figures are not only portrayed in themselves, but set against imagined visible backgrounds, and made to move amid circumstances having a pre-arranged harmony with what they do. The achievement of this, in consistency with the truth of record, is the triumph of the descriptive historian. In fictitious prose-narrative the same poetic art has still freer scope. That a lover should be leaning over a stile at one moment, and sitting under a tree at another; that it should be clear, pure moonlight when Henry is happy, and that the moon should be bowling through clouds, and a dog be heard howling at a farmhouse

near, when the same Henry means to commit suicide—
are artifices of which every ordinary novelist is master
who knows his trade. The giant Grangousier, in Rabelais, sitting by the fire, very intent upon the broiling of
some chestnuts, drawing scratches on the hearth with
the end of a burnt stick, and telling to his wife and
children pleasant stories of the days of old, is an instance of a higher kind, paralleled by many in Scott
and Cervantes. And, then, in the epic and the
drama! Hamlet with the skull in his hand, and
Homer's heroes walking by the πολυφλοίσβοιο! It is
the same throughout the whole literature of fiction:
always thought expressed and thrown off in the language of representative circumstance. Indeed, Goethe's
theory of poetical or creative literature was that it is
nothing else than the moods of its practitioners objec-
tivized as they rise. A man feels himself oppressed
and agitated by feelings and longings, now of one kind,
now of another, that have gathered upon him till they
have assumed the form of definite moral uneasiness.
If he is not a literary man, he contrives to work off the
burden, in some way or other, by the ordinary activity
of life—which, indeed, is the great preventive established by nature; but, if he is a literary man, then
the uneasiness is but the motive to creation, and the
result is a song, a drama, an epic, or a novel. Scheming
out some plan or story, which is in itself a kind of

allegory of his mood as a whole, he fills up the sketch
with minor incidents, scenes, and characters, which are
nothing more than the breaking up of the mood into
its minutiæ, and the elaboration of these minutiæ, one
by one, into the concrete. This done, the mood has
passed into the objective; it may be looked at as something external to the mind, which is therefore from
that moment rid of it, and ready for another. Such,
at least, was Goethe's theory; which, he said, would
apply most rigidly to all that he had himself written.
Nor would it be difficult, with due explanation, to
apply the theory to the works of all other masters of
creative or poetical literature. Dante may be said to
have slowly translated his whole life into one representative performance.

Several supplementary considerations must be now
adduced. The form of the poet's cogitation, we have
said, is the evolution not of *abstract propositions* but of
representative concrete circumstances. But in this, too,
there may be degrees of better and worse, of greater
and less. Precisely as, of two writers thinking in the
language of abstract speculation, we can say, without
hesitation, which has the more powerful mind, so of
two writers thinking in the other language of concrete
circumstance, one may be evidently superior to the
other. There is room, in short, for all varieties of
greater and less among poets as among other people.

Hence the folly of the attempts to exalt poetical genius, merely as such, above other kinds of intellectual manifestation. A man may be constitutionally formed so that he thinks his thoughts in the language of concrete circumstance; and still his thoughts may be very little thoughts, hardly worth having in any language. Both poets and men of science must be tried among their peers. Whether there is a common measure, and what it is; whether there is an intrinsic superiority in the mode of cogitation of the poet over that of the philosopher, or the reverse; and whether and how far we may then institute a comparison of absolute greatness between Aristotle and Homer, between Milton and Kant: these are questions of a high calculus, which most men may leave alone. There is no difficulty, however, when the question is between a Kirke White and a Kant; and when a poor poet, never so genuine in a small way, tells people that his intellect is " genius," while theirs is "talent," he runs a risk of being very unceremoniously treated.

" This palace standeth in the air,
　By necromancy placèd there,
　That it no tempest needs to fear,
　　Which way soe'er it blow it:
　And somewhat southward toward the noon
　There lies a way up to the moon,
　And thence the fairy can as soon
　　Pass to the Earth below it."

This is very sweet, and nice, and poetical (it is by Drayton, *not* a small poet, but a considerable one); and yet surely, call it genius or what you will, there was less commotion of the elements when it was produced than when Newton excogitated one of his physical theories.

We may pass to another point. The imagination following the law of the personality, some imaginations are strong where others are weak, and weak where others are strong. In other words, though all poets, as such, express themselves in the language of concrete circumstance, some are greater adepts in one kind of circumstance, others in another. Some are great in the circumstance of form, which is the sculptor's favourite circumstance; others can produce admirable compositions in *chiaroscuro;* others have the whole rainbow on their pallet. And so, some express themselves better in incident, others better in physiognomy and character. All this is recognised in daily criticism. Now, the consequence of the diversity is that it is very difficult to compare poets even amongst themselves. It is not every poet that exhibits an imagination absolutely universal, using with equal ease the language of form, of colour, of character, and of incident. Shakespeare himself, if we may infer anything from his minor poems, and from the carelessness with which he took ready-made plots for his dramas from any quarter,

was not so great a master of incident as of other kinds
of circumstance, and could hardly have rivalled Homer,
or Scott, purely as a narrative poet. How, then,
establish a comparative measure, assigning a relative
value to each kind of circumstance? How balance
what Chaucer has and has not against what Milton
has and has not—Chaucer, so skilful in physiognomy,
against Milton, who has so little of it, but who
has so much else; or how estimate the *chiaroscuro*
of Byron as against the richly coloured vegetation of
Keats? Here, too, a scientific rule is undiscoverable,
and a judgment is only possible in very decided cases,
or by the peremptory verdict of private taste.

> "Many a night I saw the Pleiads, rising thro' the
> mellow shade,
> Glitter like a swarm of fire-flies tangled in a silver
> braid."

Who will venture to institute a sure comparison of
merit between this exquisite bit of colour from Tennyson and the following simple narrative lines from the
same poet?

> " All the man was broken with remorse;
> And all his love came back a hundredfold;
> And for three hours he sobbed o'er William's child,
> Thinking of William."

There is yet a *third* thing that has to be taken into
consideration. Be a man as truly a poet as it is

possible to be, and be the kind of circumstance in
which his imagination excels as accurately known as
possible, it is not always that he can do his best.   The
poet, like other men, is subject to inequalities of mood
and feeling.   Now he is excited and perturbed, because
the occasion is one to rouse his being from its depths ;
now he is placid, calm, and commonplace.   Hence
variations in the interest of the poetical efforts of one
and the same poet.   As he cannot choose but think
poetically, whether roused or not, even the leisurely
babble of his poorest hours, if he chooses to put it
forth, will be poetical.   But he is not to be measured
by this, any more than the philosopher by his casual
trifles, or the orator by his speeches on questions that
are insignificant.   It is even important to remark that
it is only at a certain pitch of feeling that some men
become poets.   Though the essence of poetry consists in
a particular mode of *intellectual* exercise, yet the emotional moment at which different minds adopt this
mode of exercise may not be the same.   The language
of concrete circumstance is natural to *all* men when
they are very highly excited : all joy, all sorrow, all
rage, expresses itself in imaginations.   The question
then not unfrequently ought to be : At what level of
feeling does a man become or profess to be a poet ?
On this may depend, not the verdict as to the genuine-
ness of his poetry, but the disposition to spare time to

listen to it. The most assiduous members of Parliament do not feel bound to be in the House, even when a leader is speaking, unless it is on a Cabinet question or a question of some considerable interest. Some orators know this and reserve themselves; others, delighting in their profession, speak on every question. It is the same with poets, and with the same result. A Keats, though always poetical, may often be poetical with so small a stimulus that only lovers of poetry for its own sake feel themselves sufficiently interested. Why are Milton's minor poems, exquisite as they are, not cited as measures of his genius? Because they are not his speeches on Cabinet questions. Why is Spenser the favourite poet of poets, rather than a popular favourite like Byron? For the same reason that a court of law is crowded during a trial for life or death, but attended only by barristers during the trial of an intricate civil case. The subject chosen by a poetical writer is a kind of allegory of the whole state of his mental being at the moment; but some writers are not moved to allegorize so easily as others, and it is a question with readers what states of mind they care most to see allegorized. This, then, is to be taken into account, in comparing poet with poet. Precisely as an orator is remembered by his speeches on great questions, and as the position of a painter among painters is determined in part by the interest of his subjects, so in a comparison of poets, or of the same poet with himself, the seriousness of the occasion always goes for something. Shakespeare's *Venus and Adonis,* though fine as a poetical study, does not affect one with the same human interest as his plays; and there is a gradation of interest in advancing from leisurely compositions of the sweet sensuous order, such as Keats's *Endymion* and Spenser's *Faery Queene,* to the severe splendour of a *Divina Commedia* or a *Prometheus Vinctus.* True, on the one hand, poets choose their own subjects, so that these themselves are to be taken into the estimate; and, on the other, the very practice of the art of poetical expression on any subject, like the glow of the orator when he begins to speak, leads into unexpected regions. Yet, after all, in weighing a poem against others, this consideration of the emotional level at which it was produced, and of its interest in connexion with the general work and sentiment of the world, is a cause of much perplexity.

> " Sweet bird, that shunn'st the noise of folly,
>   Most musical, most melancholy !
>   Thee, chantress, oft the woods among
>   I woo, to hear thy even-song;
>   And, missing thee, I walk unseen
>   On the dry, smooth-shaven green,
>   To behold the wandering moon
>   Riding near her highest noon,
>   Like one that hath been led astray

Through the heaven's wide pathless way,
And oft, as if her head she bowed,
Stooping through a fleecy cloud.
Oft, on a plat of rising ground,
I hear the far-off curfew sound,
Over some wide-watered shore,
Swinging slow with sullen roar."

How decide between this from Milton's *Penseroso* and
this, in so different a key, from Shakespeare's *Lear*?—

" Blow, winds, and crack your cheeks ! rage ! blow !
You cataracts and hurricanoes, spout
Till you have drenched our steeples, drowned the
cocks !
You sulphurous and thought-executing fires,
Vaunt-couriers to oak-cleaving thunderbolts,
Singe my white head ! and thou, all-shaking thunder,
Strike flat the thick rotundity o' the world."

A *fourth* consideration, which intrudes itself into the
question of our appreciation of actual poetry, and which
is not sufficiently borne in mind, is that in almost
every poem there is much present besides the pure
poetry. Poetry, as such, is cogitation in the language of
concrete circumstance. Some poets excel constitutionally in one kind of circumstance, some in another ; some
are moved to this mode of cogitation on a less, others
on a greater, emotional occasion ; but, over and above
all this, it is to be noted that no poet always and
invariably cogitates in the poetical manner. Specu-

R

lation, information, mental produce and mental activity
of all kinds, may be exhibited in the course of a work
which is properly called a poem on account of its
general character; and, as men are liable to be impressed by greatness in every form wherever they
meet it, all that is thus precious in the extra-poetical
contents of a poem is included in the estimate of
the greatness of the poet. One example will suffice.
Shakespeare is as astonishing for the exuberance of
his genius in abstract notions, and for the depth of
his analytic and philosophic insight, as for the scope
and minuteness of his poetic imagination. It is as if
into a mind poetical in *form* there had been poured all
the *matter* that existed in the mind of his contemporary Bacon. In Shakespeare's plays we have thought,
history, exposition, and philosophy, all within the
round of the poet. The only difference between him
and Bacon sometimes is that Bacon writes an essay
and calls it his own, while Shakespeare writes a
similar essay and puts it into the mouth of a Ulysses
or a Polonius. It is only this fiction of a speaker
and an audience that retains many of Shakespeare's
noblest passages within the pale of strict poetry.

Hitherto we have made no formal distinction between the poet, specifically so called, and the general
practitioners of creative literature, of whatever variety.

Our examples, indeed, have been taken in the main from those whom the world recognises as poets ; but, as far as our remarks have.gone, poetry still stands synonymous with the whole literature of imagination. All who express their meaning by the literary representation of scenes, incidents, physiognomies, and characters, whether suggested by the real world or wholly imaginary, are poets. All who, doing this, do it grandly, and manifest a rich and powerful nature, are great poets. Those who excel more in the language of one kind of circumstance are poets more especially of that kind of circumstance—poets of visual scenery, poets of incident and narration, poets of physiognomy, or poets of character and sentiment, as the case may be. Those who are poetical only at a high key, and in the contemplation of themes of large human interest, are the poets who take the deepest hold on the memory of the human race. Finally, those who, having the largest amount of poetic genius, and of the best kind, associate therewith the most extensive array of other intellectual qualities, are the poets of the strongest momentum and the greatest universal chance.

Not a word in all this to exclude imaginative prose-writers. So far, Homer, Plato, Sophocles, Aristophanes, Virgil, Dante, Boccaccio, Chaucer, Cervantes, Spenser, Shakespeare, Milton, Tasso, Molière, Goethe, Richter, Scott, Defoe, and a host of others, are all huddled to-

gether, the principal figures of a great crowd, including
alike poets and prose-writers. These indeed may, in
accordance with considerations already suggested, be
distributed into groups, and that either by reference to
degree or by reference to kind. But no considerations
have yet been adduced that would separate the imaginative prose-writers, as such, from the imaginative
verse-writers, as such. Now, though this is good pro-
visionally—though it is well to keep together for a
while in the same field of view all writers of imagination, whether bards or prose-writers—yet the universal
instinct, not to say the prejudice of association and
custom, demands that the poets, as a brotherhood, shall
be more accurately defined. How, then, lead out the
poets, in the supreme sense, from the general throng
where they yet stand waiting? By what device call
the poets by themselves into the foreground, and leave
the prose-writers behind? By a union of two devices!
Go in front of the general crowd, you two : you, flag-
bearer, with your richly-painted flag, and you, fluter,
with your silver flute! Flap the flag, and let them
see it; sound the flute, and let them hear! Lo!
already the crowd wavers: it sways to and fro;
some figures seem to be pressing forward from the
midst; and at last one silver-headed old serjeant steps
out in front of all, and begins to march to the sound of
the flute. Who is it but old Homer? He is blind

and cannot see the flag; but he knows it is there, and the flute guides him. Others and others follow the patriarch, some looking to the flag, and others listening to the flute, but all marching in one direction. Shakespeare comes with the rest, stepping lightly, as if but half in earnest. And thus at last, lured by the flag and by the flute, all the poets are brought out into the foreground. The flag is *Imagery;* the flute is *Verse.* In other words, poets proper are distinguished from the general crowd of imaginative writers by a peculiar richness of language, which is called imagery, and by the use, along with that language, of a measured arrangement of words known as verse.

It is, as Mr. Dallas observes, a disputed point whether Imagery or Verse is to be regarded as the more essential element of poetry. It has been usual, of late, to give the palm to imagery. Thus, it was a remark of Lord Jeffrey—and the remark has almost passed into a proverb—that a want of relish for such rich sensuous poetry as that of Keats would argue a want of true poetical taste. The same would probably be said of Spenser. Mr. Dallas, on the other hand, thinks Verse more essential than Imagery, and in this Leigh Hunt would probably agree with him. The importance attached to a sensuous richness of language as part of poetry is, Mr. Dallas thinks, too great at present; and in opposition to Lord Jeffrey, or at least by way of corrective to his remark about Keats, he proposes that a power of appreciating such severe literary beauty as that of Sophocles shall, more than anything else, be reckoned to the credit of a man's poetical taste. Mr. Dallas, on the whole, is in the right; and this will appear more clearly if we consider what Imagery and Verse respectively are, in relation to poetry.

Imagery in poetry is secondary concrete adduced by the imagination in the expression of prior concrete. Thus, in the *simile,*—

> "The superior Fiend
> Was moving toward the shore, his ponderous shield,
> Ethereal temper, massy, large, and round,
> Behind him cast: the broad circumference
> Hung on his shoulders like the moon, whose orb
> Through optic glass the Tuscan artist views
> At evening from the top of Fesole."

Here the primary object in the imagination of the poet is Satan with his shield hung on his shoulders. While imagining this, however, the poet strikes upon a totally distinct visual appearance, that of the moon seen through a telescope, and his imagination, enamoured with the likeness, imparts the new picture to the reader as something additional to the first. Again, take the *metaphor :*—

> "Sky lowered, and, muttering thunder, some sad drops
> Wept at completing of the mortal sin
> Original."

Here the process is the same as in the simile, but more unconscious and complete. The concrete object first in the mind (so far at least as these lines are concerned) is the sky dropping rain : in the imagination of this another imagined object, that of a being shedding tears, intrudes itself ; the two objects are combined by a kind of identifying flash ; and the double concrete is presented to the reader. So, again, with that highest species of metaphor, the *personification* or *vivification*, of which, indeed, the metaphor quoted is an example.

Almost all so-called images may be reduced under one or other of the foregoing heads ; and, in any case, all imagery will be found to consist in the use of concrete to help out concrete. Now, as the very essence of the poet consists in the incessant imagination of concrete circumstance, a language rich in imagery is in itself a proof of the possession of poetical faculty in a high degree. *Cæteris paribus*, the more of subsidiary circumstance evolved in intellectual connexion with the main one the higher the evidence of poetical power. There is a likeness, in this respect, between poetical and scientific writers. Some scientific writers, *e.g.* Locke, attend so rigorously to the main thought they are pursuing as to give their style a kind of nakedness and iron straightness ; others, *e.g.* Bacon, without being indifferent to the main thought, are so full of intel-

lectual matter of all kinds that they enrich every
sentence with a *detritus* of smaller propositions related
to the one immediately on hand. So with poets.
Some poets—as Keats, Shakespeare, and Milton in
much of his poetry—so teem with concrete circumstance, or generate it so fast, as their imagination works,
that every imagined circumstance as it is put forth
from them takes with it an accompaniment of parasitic
fancies. Others, as the Greek dramatists and Dante,
sculpture their thoughts massively in severe outline.
It seems probable that the tendency to excess of imagery is natural to the Gothic or Romantic as distinct
from the Hellenic or Classical imagination ; but it is
not unlikely that the fact that poetry is now read
instead of being merely heard, as it once was, has
something to do with it. As regards the question
when imagery is excessive, *when* the richness of a poet's
language is to be called extravagance, no general principle can be laid down. The judgment on this point
in each case must depend on the particular state of
the case. A useful distinction, under this head, might
possibly be drawn between the liberty of the poet and
the duty of the artist. Keats's *Endymion* one might
safely, with reference to such a distinction, pronounce
to be too rich ; for in that poem there is no proportion
between the imagery, or accessory concrete, and the
main stem of the imagined circumstance from which

the poem derives its name. In the *Eve of St. Agnes,*
on the other hand, there is no such fault.

Of Verse, as connected with poetry, various theories
have been given. Wordsworth, whose theory is always
more narrow than his practice, makes the *rationale* of
verse to consist in this, that it provides for the mind a
succession of minute pleasurable surprises in addition
to the mere pleasure communicated by the meaning.
Others regard it as a voluntary homage of the mind
to law as law, repaid by the usual rewards of dis-
interested obedience. Mr. Dallas sets these and other
theories aside, and puts the matter on its right basis.
Verse *is* an artificial source of pleasure; it *is* an incen-
tive to attention, or a device for economizing attention;
and it *is* an act of obedience to law, if you choose so to
regard it. All these, however, are merely statements
respecting verse as something already found out and
existing; not one of them is a theory of verse in its
origin and nature. Such a theory, if it is to be sought
for at all, must clearly consist in the assertion of this,
as a fundamental fact of nature—that, when the mind
of man is either excited to a certain pitch, or engaged
in a certain kind of exercise, its actions adjust themselves, in a more express manner than usual, to time as
meted out in beats or intervals. Mr. Dallas, giving to
the statement its most transcendental form, says that
the *rationale* of metre is to be deduced from the fact

that, inasmuch as Time, according to Kant, is but a leading form of Sense, it must fall under the law of Imagination, the faculty representative of Sense. Quite independent of this philosophic generalization, which it would at least require much time to work down to the ordinary apprehension, there are many facts, some of which Mr. Dallas very acutely points out, all tending to indicate the existence of such a law as we have described. The swinging of a student to and fro in his chair during a fit of meditation, the oratorical see-saw, the evident connexion of mental states with the breathings and the pulse-beats, the power of the tick-tick of a clock to induce reverie, and of the clink-clank of a bell to make the fool think words to it, are all instances of the existence of such a law. Nay, the beginnings of poetical metre itself are to be traced in speech far on this side of what is accounted poetry. There is a visible tendency to metre in every articulate expression of strong feeling; and the ancient Greeks, we are told, used to amuse themselves with scanning passages in the speeches of their great orators.

Without trying to investigate this question farther, we would refer to a consideration connected with it which seems important for our present purpose. The law, as stated hypothetically, is that the mind, *either* when excited to a certain pitch, *or* when engaged in a particular kind of exercise, takes on a marked concordance with time as measured by beats. Now, whether is it the first or the second mental condition that necessitates this concordance? Poetry we have all along defined as a special mode of *intellectual* exercise, possible under all degrees of emotional excitement—the exercise of the mind *imaginatively,* or in the figuring forth of concrete circumstance. Is it, then, poetry as such that requires metre, or only poetry by virtue of the emotion with which it is in general accompanied—that emotion either preceding and stimulating the imaginative action, or being generated by it, as heat is evolved by friction? The question is not an easy one. On the whole, however, one might incline to the belief that, though poetry and passion have metre for their common servant, it is on passion, and not on poetry, that metre holds by original tenure. Is not metre found in its highest and most decided form in lyrical poetry, narrative poetry having less, and dramatic poetry still less of it? and wherever, in the course of a poem, there is an unusual metrical boom, is not the passage so characterized always found to be one not so much of pure concrete richness as of strong accompanying passion? What, then, if song, instead of being, as common language makes it, the complete and developed form of poetry, should have to be scientifically defined as the complete and developed form of oratory, passing into poetry only

in as far as passion, in its utterance, always seizes and
whirls with it shreds and atoms of imagined circumstance ?   If this is the true theory, Verse belongs, by
historical origin, to Oratory, and lingers with Poetry
only as an entailed inheritance.

Prose, then, *may*, as we have said, make inroads upon
that region of the literature of the concrete which has
hitherto been under the dominion of verse. But, on the
other hand, verse, whatever it may have been in its origin,
exists now, like many other sovereignties, by right of
expediency, constitutional guarantee, and the voluntary
submission of those who are its subjects.   And here
it is that the theories of Wordsworth and others have
their proper place.   They are theories of verse, not in
its origin, but in its character as an existing institution
in the literature of the concrete.   They tell us what we
can now do intellectually by means of verse which we
could not do if her royalty were abolished.   They point
to the fact that in literature, as in other departments of
activity, law and order, and even the etiquette of artificial ceremonial, though they may impose intolerable
burdens on the disaffected and the boorish, are but conditions of liberty and development to all higher, and
finer, and more cultured natures.   In short (and this is
the important fact), metre, rhyme, and the like, are not
only devices for the sweet and pleasant conveyance
of the poet's meaning after it is formed ; they are

devices assisting beforehand in the creation of that meaning. They are devices so spurring and delighting the imagination, while they chafe and restrain it, that its thoughts and combinations in the world of concrete circumstance are more rich, more rare, more occult, more beautiful, than they would otherwise be. Like the effect of the music on the fountain and the company of Bacchanals in Tennyson's strange vision is the effect of verse on poetical thought:

> "Then methought I heard a mellow sound,
>   Gathering up from all the lower ground;
>   Narrowing in to where they sat assembled,
>   Low, voluptuous music winding trembled,
>   Wov'n in circles: they that heard it sigh'd,
>   Panted hand in hand with faces pale,
>   Swung themselves, and in low tones replied,
>   Till the fountain spouted, showering wide
>   Sleet of diamond-drift and pearly hail."

Here we must stop our discussion of the Theory of Poetry. For much that we have left undiscussed, and especially for a philosophical division of poetry according to its kinds, we must refer to Mr. Dallas. We recommend his book highly and cordially. There is perhaps a stronger dash of what may be called Okenism in his style of speculation than some readers may like: as, for example, in his systematic laying out of everything into corresponding threes or triads. Poetry

figures throughout this treatise as a compound result
of three laws—the laws of unconsciousness, the law of
harmony, and the law of imagination; which laws are
supreme respectively in three kinds of poetry—lyrical
poetry, epic poetry, and dramatic poetry; which three
kinds of poetry, again, correspond historically with
Eastern, primitive, or divine art, Grecian, antique, or
classical art, and Western, modern, or romantic art;
which historical division, again, corresponds philoso-
phically with such trinities as these—I, he, thou; time
future, time past, time present; immortality, God,
freedom; the good, the true, the beautiful. All this,
stated thus abruptly and without explanation, may
seem hopeless matter to some; but even they will find
in the book much that will please them, in the shape
of shrewd observation and lucid and deep criticism,
valuable on its own account, and very different from
what used to be supplied to the last age by *its*
critics.

VI.

PROSE AND VERSE: DE QUINCEY.

VI.

PROSE AND VERSE: DE QUINCEY.[1]

In the Preface to this series of volumes (which is intended to be a more perfect accomplishment, under the author's own editorship, of a scheme of literary collection already executed very creditably by an American publisher) Mr. De Quincey ventures on something rather unusual. He ventures on a theoretical classification of his own writings for the benefit of critics. The following is the passage in which he states this classification and the grounds of it :—

"Taking as the basis of my remarks the collective American edition, I will here attempt a rude general classification of all the articles which compose it. I distribute them grossly into three classes :—

"*First*, into that class which proposes primarily to amuse the reader ; but which, in doing so, may or may not happen occasionally to reach a higher station, at which the amusement passes into an impassioned interest. Some papers are merely playful ; but others

---

[1] *British Quarterly Review*, July, 1854.—"Selections Grave and Gay, from Writings published and unpublished." By Thomas De Quincey. Vols. I. and II., containing "Autobiographic Sketches." Edinburgh, 1853–4.

have a mixed character.   These present *Autobiographic Sketches* illustrate what I mean.   Generally, they pretend to little beyond that sort of amusement which attaches to any real story, thoughtfully and faithfully related, moving through a succession of scenes sufficiently varied, that are not suffered to remain too long upon the eye, and that connect themselves at every stage with intellectual objects.   But, even here, I do not scruple to claim from the reader, occasionally, a higher consideration.   At times, the narrative rises into a far higher key. . . .

   "Into the *second* class I throw those papers which address themselves purely to the understanding as an insulated faculty, or do so primarily.   Let me call them by the general name of essays.   These, as in other cases of the same kind, must have their value measured by two separate questions.   A.—What is the problem, and of what rank in dignity or use, which the essay undertakes?   And next—that point being settled—B.—What is the success obtained? and (as a separate question) What is the executive ability displayed in the solution of the problem?   This latter question is naturally no question for myself, as the answer would involve a verdict upon my own merit.   But, generally, there will be quite enough in the answer to Question A for establishing the value of any essay on its soundest basis.   *Prudens interrogatio est dimidium scientiæ:* skilfully to frame your question is half-way towards insuring the true answer.   Two or three of the problems treated in these essays I will here rehearse [Mr. De Quincey here cites, as examples of the kind of writings which he refers to the second

class, his essays on the following subjects :—*Essenism,
The Cæsars,* and *Cicero*]. These specimens are sufficient
for the purpose of informing the reader that I do not
write without a thoughtful consideration of my subject;
and, also, that to think reasonably upon any question has
never been allowed by me as a sufficient ground for writing upon it, unless I believed myself able to offer some
considerable novelty. Generally, I claim (not arrogantly,
but with firmness) the merit of rectification applied to
absolute errors, or to injurious limitations of the truth.

"Finally, as a third class, and, in virtue of their aim,
as a far higher class of compositions, included in the
American collection, I rank *The Confessions of an
Opium-Eater,* and also (but more emphatically) the
Suspiria de Profundis. On these, as modes of impassioned prose, ranging under no precedents that I
am aware of in any literature, it is much more difficult
to speak justly, whether in a hostile or a friendly character. As yet neither of these two works has ever
received the least degree of that correction and pruning
which both require so extensively ; and of the *Suspiria*
not more than perhaps one-third has yet been printed.
When both have been fully revised, I shall feel myself
entitled to ask for a more determinate adjudication on
their claims as works of art. At present I feel author-
ized to make haughtier pretensions in right of their
conception than I shall venture to do under the peril
of being supposed to characterize their *execution.* Two
remarks only I shall address to the equity of my reader.
First, I desire to remind him of the perilous difficulty
besieging all attempts to clothe in words the visionary
scenes derived from the world of dreams, where a single

false note, a single word in a wrong key, ruins the whole music; and, secondly, I desire him to consider the utter sterility of universal literature in this one department of impassioned prose—which certainly argues some singular difficulty, suggesting a singular duty of indulgence in criticising any attempt that even imperfectly succeeds. The sole Confessions, belonging to past times, that have at all succeeded in· engaging the attention of men, are those of St. Austin and of Rousseau. The very idea of breathing a record of human passion, not into the ear of the random crowd, but of the saintly confessional, argues an impassioned theme. Impassioned, therefore, should be the tenor of the composition. Now, in St. Augustine's Confessions is found one most impassioned passage—viz., the lamentation for the death of his youthful friend in the fourth book; one, and no more. Farther, there is nothing. In Rousseau there is not even so much. In the whole work there is nothing grandly affecting but the character and the inexplicable misery of the writer."

No one acquainted with Mr. De Quincey's writings will deny the soundness and the completeness of this classification; nor do we think that a critic, proposing to himself so ambitious a task as an appreciation of Mr. De Quincey's genius as a whole, could do better than quietly assume it, and proceed to examine Mr. De Quincey's merits, first as a writer of interesting memoirs, secondly, as an essayist or elucidator of difficult historical and other problems, and, lastly, as an almost

unique practitioner of a peculiar style of imaginative or
highly impassioned prose. Such an examination, conducted never so rigorously, if by a competent person,
would confirm the impression, now entertained on all
hands, that among the most remarkable names in the
history of English literature for many a day must be
ranked that of Thomas De Quincey. *Our* purpose,
however, is by no means so extensive. We do not
mean to comment on Mr. De Quincey as a writer of
memoirs and narratives, nor to cull from his numerous
contributions in that department—the present two
volumes included—any of the delightful reminiscences
with which they abound. We do not mean, either, to
follow Mr. De Quincey through any of the various
tracks of speculation into which his pure intellectual
activity has led him, and thus to exhibit the delicacy
and subtlety of his thinking faculty, the range of his
observation and knowledge, and the value of his conclusions on obscure and vexed questions. In this
department, we believe, he would be found fully
entitled to the praise which he has claimed for himself—the praise of having been practically faithful to
that theory of literature which maintains that no man
is entitled to write upon a subject merely by having
something reasonable to say about it, unless that something is also, to some extent, new. It is with Mr. De
Quincey, however, in the last of the three aspects in

which he has presented himself to notice in the foregoing passage that we propose exclusively to concern ourselves.   We thank Mr. De Quincey for having so presented himself.   Not only, in so doing, has he indicated, with all due modesty, what he esteems his peculiar and characteristic place in English literature, and the scene and nature of his highest triumphs as a writer ; he has also, at the same time, suggested a very curious subject for critical discussion.

By the established custom of all languages, there is a great interval between the mental state accounted proper in prose writing and that allowed, and even required, in verse.   A man, for the most part, would be ashamed of permitting himself in prose the same freedom of intellectual whimsy, the same arbitrariness of combination, the same riot of imagery, the same care for the exquisite in sound and form, perhaps even the same depth and fervour of feeling, that he would exhibit unabashed in verse.   There is an idea that, if the matter lying in the mind waiting for expression is of a very select and rare kind, or if the mood is peculiarly fine and elevated, a writer must quit the platform of prose, and ascend into the region of metre.   To use a homely figure, the feeling is that, in such circumstances, one must not remain in the plainly-furnished apartment on the ground-floor where ordinary business is transacted, but must step up-stairs to the place of elegance and leisure. Take, for example, the following passage from *Comus :—*

> " Sabrina fair,
>   Listen where thou art sitting,
> Under the glassy, cool, translucent wave,
>   In twisted briads of lilies knitting
> The loose train of thy amber-dropping hair ;
>   Listen for dear honour's sake,
>   Goddess of the silver lake—
>   Listen and save."

If any man, having preconceived exactly the tissue of meaning involved in this passage, had tried to express it in prose, he would have had a sense of shame in doing so, and would have run the risk of being regarded as a coxcomb. Only in verse will men consent, in general, to receive such specimens of the intellectually exquisite ; but offer them never so tiny a thing of the kind in verse, and they are not only satisfied, but charmed. Nor is it only with regard to the peculiarly exquisite, or the peculiarly luscious in meaning, that this is true ; it is true, also, to a certain extent, of the peculiarly sublime, or the peculiarly magnificent. Thus Samson, soliloquizing on his blindness—

> " The vilest here excel me ;
> They creep, yet see : I, dark, in light exposed
> To daily fraud, contempt, abuse, and wrong ;

Within doors, or without, still as a fool
In power of others, never in my own;
Scarce half I seem to live, dead more than half.
O dark, dark, dark ; amid the blaze of noon
Irrecoverably dark, total eclipse,
Without all hope of day !
O, first-created beam, and thou great Word,
Let there be light, and light was over all ;
Why am I thus bereaved thy prime decree ?
The sun to me is dark
And silent as the moon,
When she deserts the night,
Hid in her vacant interlunar cave."

In prose something equivalent to this might have been
permitted by reason of the severe impressiveness of the
theme ; but, to render the entire mass of thoughts and
images acceptable precisely as they are, without re-
trenchment or toning down, one almost requires to see
the golden cincture of the enclasping verse.   Take a
passage where, this cincture having been purposely removed in the process of translation, the sheer meaning
may be seen by itself in a prose-heap.   The following is
a description from Æschylus, literally translated :—

" So Tydeus, raving and greedy for the fight, wars
like a serpent in its hissings beneath the noon-tide heat,
and he smites the sage seer, son of Oïcleus, with a
taunt, saying that he is crouching to death and battle
out of cowardice.   Shouting out such words as these,
he shakes their shadowy crests, the hairy honours of

his helm, while beneath his buckler bells cast in brass
are shrilly pealing terror. On his buckler, too, he has
this arrogant device—a gleaming sky tricked out with
stars, and in the centre a brilliant full moon conspicuous,
most august of the heavenly bodies, the eye of night.
Chafing thus in his vaunting harness, he wars beside
the bank of the river, enamoured of conflict, like a steed
champing his bit with rage, that rushes forth when he
hears the voice of the trumpet."

Knowing that this is translated from verse, we admire
it ; but, if it were presented to us as an original effort of
description in prose, we should, though still admiring it,
feel that it went beyond bounds. What we should feel
would be, not that such a description ought not to be
given, but that prose is not good enough and leisurely
enough to have the honour of containing it. And,
so, generally, when a man launches forth in a grand
strain, or when he begins to put forth matter more
than usually rich and luscious, our disposition is to
interrupt him and persuade him to exchange the style
for that of metre. " Had we not better step up-stairs ? "
is virtually what we say on such occasions ; and this not
ironically, but with a view to hear out what has to be
said with greater pleasure. In short, we allow all
ordinary business of a literary kind—plain statement,
equable narrative, profound investigation, strong direct
appeal—to be transacted in prose ; we even permit a
moderate amount of beauty, of enthusiasm, and of ima-

ginative play, to intermingle with the current of prose-composition; but there is a point, marked either by the unusual fineness of the matter of thought, its unusual arbitrariness and luxuriance, its unusual grandeur, or its unusually impassioned character, at which, by a law of custom, a man must either consent to be silent, or must lift himself into verse. On such occasions it is as when a speaker is expected to leave his ordinary place in the body of the house and mount the tribune.

There is an element in the philosophy of this matter which it may be well to attend to before going farther. We have spoken as if the meaning to be uttered were generally already in the mind before the form of utterance is chosen. We have represented the case as if there were already internally prepared by a writer a certain tissue or series of thoughts and images, and as if it were then capable of being made a deliberate question whether he should emit the intellectual whole thus prepared in metre or in prose. But this is not the actual state of the fact. The actual fact is that the meaning that will in any case exist to be expressed is conditioned beforehand by the form of expression selected—in other words, that the matter cogitated does not precede the form of expression and engage this or that form of expression at its option, but that the form of expression assists from the outset in determining the kind of matter that shall be cogitated. This removes a

practical difficulty. A man who writes in prose is, by
the fact that he does so, kept within the bounds of prose
in the character of his mental combinations. Those
peculiar finenesses and flights of intellectual activity
which are native to verse are then simply not developed.
His thoughts stop short precisely at that point of richness, quaintness, or luxuriance, where prose ceases to be
prose. That this point will vary according to a writer's
taste and faculty does not for the present matter. On
the other hand, the writer who uses metre and rhyme
does not prosecute his train of meaning independently
of them, but partly by their very aid in leading him this
way or that. A man who has made up his mind to add
to all the other conditions of his thinking these two—
first, that he shall think in synchronism with certain
metrical beats, and, secondly, that he shall think forward
to that point in his mental horizon where he sees the
glimmer of a certain predetermined rhyme—such a
writer necessarily accustoms himself to a more complex
law of cogitation than rules the prose-writer, and moves
through an atmosphere of more arbitrary and exquisite
and occult suggestions. This may look mechanical;
but it is the very *rationale* of verse and its functions.
Versifiers are men who have voluntarily, in accordance
with some original bent in their nature, submitted their
thoughts to a more complex mechanism than ordinary
prose-writers, and whose reward is that, when they are

such masters of the mechanism as no longer to think of
its existence, they can revel in combinations more intimate, extreme, and exquisite than their prose thoughts
would be. In reading a passage of verse, therefore, we
have to bear in mind that the meaning came in part to
be what it is because the verse assisted to create it.
Thus, in the passage quoted from *Comus*, it is unnecessary to trouble ourselves with fancying what reception
such a dainty little picture would have met with if
offered originally in prose; for it is what it is simply
because metre and rhyme conspired in the production
of it. So, also, in the passage from *Samson Agonistes*,
the mass of thoughts and images would have stood
somewhat different from the first, had it not been
shaped implicitly to fill the mould of the precise metre.
Again, in the description from Æschylus, whatever
passes the degree of imaginative richness deemed suitable to prose is justified by the recollection that these
excesses were perpetrated in verse.

This last instance suggests an observation of some
importance. It may happen, and does often happen,
that the metrical form may have been necessary to the
evolution of a particular piece of meaning, and may yet
not be so necessary to the preservation and perpetuation
of it, after it has been produced. Only under the condition of metre may a thought of special splendour or
beauty have been actually produced; and yet, once it

is fairly on this side of the Styx, the metrical mould
necessary for its safe conveyance hither may be frac-
tured, and the thought will still stand appreciable on
its own merits. And thus it is that much of the greatness of the highest poetry is indestructible by even the
rudest process of transmutation into literal prose. The
actual matter of Homer's *Iliad* and of the great Greek
tragedies might never have existed but for the suggestive power in the minds of the poets of those precise
hexameters and iambic and choral measures in which
it was imagined and delivered; but much of what is
noble in it survives yet in the baldest prose translation.
The preciousness of the thought is to be recognised
even after the fabric of the verse has been crumbled
into the mere form of unmetrical powder.

All this, however, does not affect the practical importance of the fact that custom has established a
distinction between what is lawful in prose and what
is lawful in verse. True, for the reasons above stated,
the distinction causes no one any personal inconvenience. He who prefers to write in prose does so because
he finds he can make prose sufficient. The necessity
for writing in verse exists only where there is the prior
habit, if we may so call it, of thinking in verse. When
the thoughts of a prose-writer reach a degree of exquisiteness, or lusciousness, or imaginative grandeur, at
which prose refuses to contain them, nature provides

the remedy by simply whirling him into verse. He has the option of allowing himself to be so whirled, or of restraining himself, and refusing to go on whenever the said point is reached. He may choose never "to go up-stairs," never to put himself into such a strain that it shall be necessary for him to ascend the tribune in order to speak. But here lies the question. Where *is* that ideal point at which a man must either smother what is in his mind or ascend the tribune and speak in verse? What are the limits and capabilities of prose; and through what series of gradations does prose pass into technical and completed verse? If a man refuses to be whirled past the extreme prose point, what amount of farther intellectual possibility, and of what precise kinds, does he thus forego? Is the ulterior region into which verse admits co-extensive with that which it leaves behind; and, if not, what is its measure? Does it overhang the realm of prose like a superior ether, nearer the empyrean, or does it only softly round it to a small measurable distance? Is the relation of prose to verse that of absolute inferiority, or of inferiority in some respects counterbalanced by superiority in others? In short, what is it that verse can do and prose cannot, and what is the value of this special kind of intellectual work which only verse can transact? We have spoken vaguely of the boundary between prose and verse as being marked by a certain degree of fineness, or ex-

quisiteness, or occultness, or lusciousness, or arbitrariness, or grandeur, or passionateness, in the matter of
thought to be expressed; but we must now seek for a
more exact definition, so as to see what proportion of
just human thought prose at its utmost will contain,
and what residue must either be foregone or relegated
to verse.

It will be admitted that for all the purposes of what
is called investigation, speculation, generalization, philosophical discussion and exposition, prose is sufficient.
There is no need for a man "to step up-stairs" so long
as he deals with matter pertaining to what is called
the pure understanding. A Kant, a Leibnitz, or a Sir
William Hamilton, so far as their pure reasonings are concerned, need never find themselves whirled past the prose
point, notwithstanding that the matters about which
their reasoning is employed may be the generalities on
which the universe rests, and that their conclusions in
such matters may be the result of vast force of intellect,
and may set the whole world in amaze. The actual
reasonings of even a half-inspired Plato may be delivered to their last link without the aid of verse. This,
then, is much to say in behalf of poor prose. It ought
to silence the absurd chatter of many a versifier, exulting in his technick without any just knowledge of what
it really is. The large world-shaking abstraction, the
profound of all-penetrating stroke of intellect, the rich

shower of fructifying propositions, the iron chain of
conquering syllogisms: all these are possible to the
prose-writer in a manner and to an extent beyond the
legitimate or usual powers of verse. The verse of a
Shakespeare, it is true, will teem with matter secreted
by the purely intellectual organ, the same being so
interfused with the poetic that the superfluity does
not seem a fault ; and a Wordsworth may, in beautiful
metre, reproduce the philosophizings of a Spinoza. But
even those masters of verse could do nothing in this
department by the help of their iambics which equal
power could not have done more rigorously and sys-
tematically with the iambics away. In passing into
verse, the poet may take such matter with him ; but he
must treat it in such a way that, from the point of
view of the pure thinker, there is a loss of the logical
virtue. With all the reverence that exists for verse as
distinct from prose, no one will deny that at the present
moment there lies imbedded in the prose-treatises of
the world a mass of most precious substance distinct
from all that can be found in verse.

Again, prose is sufficient for the expression of at
least a large proportion of all possible human feeling.
It would be difficult to say at what pitch of mere feeling it would be absolutely necessary to go "up-stairs"
for the means of adequate expression. Joy, sorrow,
indignation, rage, love, hatred—there is ample scope

for the expression of these passions within the limits
of prose. Impassioned prose oratory can show as
splendid renderings of some of these passions as any
that can be found in verse. Indeed there are some
passions—as, for example, those of laughter and indignation—which find a more natural utterance in prose.
And yet it is precisely in this matter of the expression of feeling or passion that we first come in sight
of the natural origin of metre. At a certain pitch of
fervour or feeling the voice does instinctively lift itself
into song. Intense grief breaks into a wail, great joy
bursts into a measured shout, pride moves to a slow
march; all extreme passion tends to cadence. "And
the king was much moved, and went up to the
chamber over the gate and wept; and, as he went, thus
he said, Oh, my son Absalom, my son, my son Absalom! Would God I had died for thee; Oh, Absalom,
my son, my son!" Wherever there is emotion like
this, we have a rudimentary metre in its expression;
and verse in all its forms is nothing else than the pro-
longation and extended ingenious application of this
hint of nature. It may be laid down as a principle,
therefore, that *impassioned* writing tends to the metrical, and that, though this tendency may gratify itself
to a great length within the limits of such wild
metrical prose as it will itself create for the passing
occasion, yet at a certain point in all feelings, and

T

more particularly in such feelings as joy, sorrow, and love, it will overleap the boundary of what in any sense can be called prose, and will seize on that artifice of verse which past custom has provided and consecrated. Walking by the river-side, full of thought and sadness, even the homely rustic minstrel will find it natural to pour forth his feelings to the established cadence of some well-known melody :—

> " But minstrel Burn cannot assuage
>   His woes while time endureth,
>   To see the changes of this age,
>   Which fleeting Time procureth :
>   Full many a place stands in hard case
>   Where joy was wont beforrow,
>   With Humes that dwelt on Leader braes,
>   And Scotts that dwelt on Yarrow."

Here the very tune of the thought seems to keep time with the arm as it moves the bow of an imaginary violin. And so with more modern and more cultured poets. Thus Tennyson :—

> " Break, break, break,
>   On thy cold grey stones, O sea !
>   And I would that my tongue could utter
>   The thoughts that arise in me !
>
>   O, well for the fisherman's boy,
>   That he shouts with his sister at play ;
>   O, well for the sailor-lad,
>   That he sings in his boat on the bay.

And the stately ships go on
    To their haven under the hill ;
But O for the touch of a vanished hand,
    And the sound of a voice that is still !

Break, break, break,
    At the foot of thy crags, O sea !
But the tender grace of a day that is dead
    Will never come back to me."

This is not a case in which the same feeling, to the same intensity, could have been expressed in any form of metrical prose, and in which, therefore, the verse is only adopted to increase the beauty of the form ; it is a case in which the feeling had to overleap the bounds of possible prose, on pain of being mutilated.

There remains now only the field of representative literature, the literature of the concrete. How far does prose stretch over this field ; and what portion of it, if any, is the exclusive possession of verse ? The field divides itself theoretically into two halves or sections—the domain of mere history and description, in which the business of the writer is with the actual concrete, the actual scenes and events of the world ; and the high domain of imagination or fiction, in which the business of the writer is with concrete furnished forth by his own creative phantasy.

Is prose sufficient for all the purposes of historical or descriptive writing, viewed as separately as may

T 2

be from that department of imaginative writing into
which it shades off so gradually ?   We should say
that it is.   For all the purposes of exact record, of
exact reproduction of fact in all its vast variety of
kinds—fact of scenery, fact of biography, fact of
history, fact even of transacted passion—prose is
sufficient, and verse unnecessary, or even objectionable.
For the true and accurate retention and representation
of all that man can observe (and a large and splendid
function this is) prose is superior to verse ; and, when
this function is committed to verse, there is an inevitable sacrifice of the pure aim of the function, though
that sacrifice may at times be attended with the gain of
something supposed to be better.   That this statement
may not be immediately assented to will arise from
a confusion of the descriptive and the imaginative.
Thomson's *Seasons* and much of Wordsworth's poetry
are called descriptive compositions ; but, properly
considered, they are not records, but the imaginative
use of records.   Again, Homer is a narrative poet ;
but narration with him is but a special use of the
imaginative faculty.   Isolate strictly the department
of historical or descriptive writing proper from that
into which it so readily shades off, and prose is the
legitimate king of it.   We can conceive but two
apparent exceptions—first, where verse itself is one
of the facts to be recorded ; and, secondly, where the

historian or the describer waxes so warm in the act
of description that he approaches the singing point.
In the first case, verse must be treated as any other
fact; that is, it must be represented accurately by
being quoted—which, however, is a prose feat. In the
second case, it is not the facts that the historian sings,
but his own impassioned feeling about them: a matter
already provided for under another head.

And now for the real tug of war. What are the
relative capabilities of Prose and Verse in the great
field of fictitious or imaginative literature? It is
needless to say that here it is that, by the universal
impression of mankind, Verse is allowed the superior
rank of the two sisters. The very language we use
implies this. The word *poetry* literally means creation
or fiction, and is thus co-extensive with the whole
field of literature under notice. And yet it is by a
deviation from the common usage of speech that we
use the word poetry in this its wide etymological
sense. When we speak of a poet, we mean, unless
we indicate otherwise, a man who writes in verse;
when we speak of English poetry, we mean the
library of English books written in verse. This is
significant. It indicates the belief that the essential
act of ποίησις is somehow connected with the metrical
tendency, and best transacts itself in alliance with
that tendency. In other words, it implies a conviction

that, when the mind sets itself to work in that peculiar manner which we designate by the term imagination or imaginative exercise, the assumption of the metrical form of expression is natural, and perhaps in some cases essential, to it. And yet this is contradicted at once, to some extent, by palpable fact. In the prose literature of all languages there is a vast proportion of works in which the prevailing intention of the authors is that of strict ποίησις, the strict invention and elaboration of an imaginary or fictitious concrete. There is the novel; there is the prose romance; there is a prose literature of imagination in various forms. *Robinson Crusoe, Don Quixote,* the *Waverley Novels,* are prose efforts of a kind as strictly falling under the head of ποίησις or creation, in its widest sense, as the *Prometheus Vinctus, Paradise Lost,* or Tennyson's *Princess.* Accordingly, we do sometimes rank the writers of imaginative prose among poets or "makers." The question, then, arises : can we, by philosophical investigation, or by the examination of actual instances, determine in what precise conditions it is that the generic act of ποίησις, or imaginative exercise, disdains the level ground of prose, and even its highest mountain-tops, and rises instinctively and necessarily on the wings of verse ?

There are various kinds of ποίησις, or imaginative exercise, according to the species of concrete imagined.

There is the ποίησις of mere inanimate objects and
scenery, as in much of Thomson; there is the ποίησις
of physiognomy and costume, as in much of Scott and
Chaucer; there is the ποίησις of incident and action,
as in narrative poetry; there is the ποίησις of feelings
and states of mind, as in songs; there is, as an extension
of this last, the ποίησις of character. From the
masterly exercise of these different kinds of ποίησις
in different forms of combination arise the great
kinds of poetry—the descriptive, the epic, the dramatic, and the lyric. But out of this objective
classification of the varieties of imaginative exercise
can we derive the clue we seek? At first sight not.
If Thomson and Wordsworth describe imaginary scenes
in verse, so do Dickens and Scott and a thousand
others in prose; if we have admirable delineations of
physiognomy and costume in the *Canterbury Pilgrimage,* so also have we in the *Waverley Novels;* if the
Iliad is an effort of narrative imagination, so also is
Don Quixote; if feelings and characters are represented
in song and the Iambic drama, so are they also in
prose fiction. And yet, as was hinted at the outset,
there does seem to be a condition of the matter
imagined such that prose will not generally contain
and convey that matter. What is that condition?
The instances cited at the outset served vaguely to
indicate it. In the quotation from Milton, and in

that from Æschylus, it was felt that there was something in the actual matter presented by the passages
that would have had to be parted with if the medium
had been prose. Thus, in the first passage, it was
felt that the image of Sabrina

> " Under the glassy, cool, translucent wave,
>   In twisted braids of lilies knitting
> The loose train of her amber-dropping hair,"

was too dainty for prose. Again, in the passage from
Æschylus, it was felt that the description in the following sentence would have sustained some reduction if
the composition had originally been in the prose form :

> " On his buckler, too, he had this arrogant device—a
> gleaming sky tricked out with stars, and in the centre
> a brilliant full moon conspicuous (most august of the
> heavenly bodies, the eye of night)."

Prose might have given all of this as far as the paren-
thesis, but there it would have stopped.

So far as we had come to any conclusion from these
instances as to the precise character of that concrete
which prose instinctively refuses to carry, and which is
yet welcome if it is presented in verse, we defined it
as consisting in a certain unusual degree of richness,
lusciousness, exquisiteness, arbitrariness, occultness,
grandeur, or passionateness.   We will now limit the
catalogue. of qualities to these two, richness and arbi-

trariness; and we will aver, as an approximation to the truth, that the character of a combination by the imaginative faculty which determines that it must take place in verse is either an unusual degree of richness or an unusual degree of arbitrariness. This may not appear to reserve for verse a sufficient monopoly of the great intellectual function of ποίησις; but, duly interpreted, it will be found to correspond with the fact. It is not, we believe, the mere grandeur or magnificence of a phantasy, it is not its mere fineness, or delicacy, or exquisiteness, that *necessarily* renders prose incapable of it; it is chiefly its richness, or its arbitrariness. The limits of prose as regards the quality of passionateness have already been suggested under a former head. What we call an "impassioned imagination" is a mixed thing, consisting of an objective phantasy, with a peculiar subjective mood breathed through it : it is ποίησις in conjunction with πάθησις; and, having already considered when it is that πάθησις breaks out into singing, we are now concerned only with the distinct inquiry at what point, if at any, ποιησις itself insists on becoming metrical.

In the first place, then, there is a peculiar *richness* of literary concrete of which prose seems to be incapable. By richness of concrete we mean very much what is meant by excess of imagery. Let there be a splendid single combination of the poetical faculty—a splendid

imaginary scene, a splendid imaginary incident or
action, a splendid imaginary state of feeling or
character—and prose will surely and easily compass
it. The severe story of a Greek drama may be told
in outline in noble prose; nay, each incident in such
a drama may be rendered in a prose narrative so
as to be impressive and effective. The visual fancy
of the blind Earl and his guide on the cliff at Dover,
or of Milton's Satan alighting on the orb of the sun
and darkening it like a telescopic spot, may also be
outlined in prose so as finely to affect the imagination. And so, universally, a single imagined circumstance, however grand, or a moderately sparse tissue
of imagined circumstances, may be delivered in prose.
But, when the outline is thickly filled in with
imagery; when, in the expression of the main circumstance already imagined, masses of subsidiary circumstance are adduced; when the stem of the original
poetic thought does not proceed straight and shaft-
like, but is clustered round with rich parasitic fancies:
then prose begins to despair. Thus, in Alexander
Smith's image descriptive of the commencement of a
friendship between one youth, the speaker, and another
whom he admired:—

> " An opulent soul
> Dropt in my path like a great cup of gold,
> All rich and rough with stories of the gods."

Here the main fancy, the cup of gold dropped in the youth's path, is perfectly within the compass of imaginative prose; but only a daring prose-writer would have turned the cup so lovingly to show its chasing—or, as we say, would have so dallied with the image. Again, in the fine stanza from Keats's *Eve of St. Agnes :—*

> "And still she slept an azure-lidded sleep,
> In blanched linen, smooth, and lavender'd ;
> While he from forth the closet brought a heap
> Of candied apple, quince, and plum, and gourd ;
> With jellies soother than the creamy curd,
> And lucent syrops, tinct with cinnamon ;
> Manna and dates, in argosy transferred,
> From Fez ; and spiced dainties, every one,
> From silken Samarcand to cedar'd Lebanon."

In some very luscious prose, such as we find in the *Arabian Nights*, we might have had the picture as elaborately finished, and even the same express catalogue of dainties ; but one or two of the touches of subsidiary circumstance, as in the first, seventh, and last lines, would have been almost certainly omitted. Again, much more visibly, in the following passage from *Paradise Lost*, describing Satan defying Gabriel and his host of warrior-angels.

> " While thus he spake, the angelic squadron bright
> Turned fiery red, sharpening in mooned horns

Their phalanx, and began to hem him round
With ported spears, as thick as when a field
Of Ceres, ripe for harvest, waving bends
Her bearded grove of ears, which way the wind
Sways them : the careful ploughman doubting stands,
Lest on the threshing-floor his hopeful sheaves
Prove chaff.   On the other side, Satan alarmed,
Collecting all his might, dilated stood,
Like Teneriffe, or Atlas, unremoved :
His stature reached the sky, and on his crest
Sat Horror plumed."

Here, it is obvious, verse has left prose caught in the
thicket.   The main circumstance could have been
represented in prose ; and prose might have dared
one or two of the strokes of subsidiary imagination ;
but such a profusion of simile and metaphor in so
short a space would have bewildered and encumbered
it.   And so, generally, we may consider it as made
out that prose is incapable of so rich a literary concrete as verse may justly undertake, and that, where
prose deals with pure poetic matter, a certain comparative thinness or sparseness is requisite in the
texture of that matter, however bold or fine or grand
may be the separate imaginations which compose it.
Hence it is, we think, that ancient classical poetry,
and especially Greek epic and dramatic poetry, is
more capable, as a whole, of retaining its impressiveness when translated into prose than most modern

poetry when similarly treated. The ancient poetry was more severe, delighting in imaginations clearly and separately sculptured ; the modern muse favours richness of subsidiary imagery, and delights in ornamenting even its largest creations with minute tracery.

In the second place, a certain degree of *arbitrariness* in an imaginative combination seems to place it beyond the capacity of ordinary prose. Our meaning will be best seen by an example or two. When Shelley says,

> " Life, like a dome of many-coloured glass,
>   Stains the white radiance of eternity,"

he presents to the mind a singularly beautiful image or combination, which is at once accepted and enjoyed. Yet it is a combination so different from anything likely to have suggested itself to the logical understanding, or even to the imagination as swayed and directed by the logical understanding, that we question if it could have been arrived at but for that extraordinary nimbleness in seizing remote analogies which is communicated to the mind when it thinks under the complex law of metre. A prose-writer of great imaginative power will often strike out combinations of a high degree of arbitrariness, but rarely will he feel himself entitled to such an

excursion into the occult as the above. So, also, in
the following passage from Keats :—

> " O Sorrow !
> Why dost borrow
> The natural hue of health from vermeil lips ?
> To give maiden blushes
> To the white-rose bushes ?
> Or is it thy dewy hand the daisy tips ?
>
> O Sorrow !
> Why dost borrow
> The lustrous passion from a falcon-eye ?
> To give the glow-worm light ?
> Or, on a moonless night,
> To tinge, on siren shores, the salt sea-spry ?"

Here, also, the links of association between idea and
idea seem to be too occult, and the entire tissue of
images too arbitrary, for prose to have produced a
passage exactly equivalent; and yet, as it is presented
to us in verse, we have no doubt as to the legitimacy
of the combination, and are thankful for it. And the
reason again is that the mind, rising and falling on
the undulation of metre—poised, so to speak, on
metrical wings—is enabled to catch more fantastic and
airy analogies, and to dart to greater distances with
less sense of difficulty, than when pacing never so
majestically the *terra firma* of prose. The following
from Tennyson is a fine instance of the same :—

> " The splendour falls on castle walls,
>   And snowy summits old in story ;
> The long light shakes across the lakes,
>   And the wild cataract leaps in glory.
> Blow, bugle, blow ; set the wild echoes flying:
> Answer, echoes, answer—dying, dying, dying."

Here is a combination the coherence of which is felt by every imaginative mind, and which possesses a singular representative, as distinct from mere expository, power; and yet it almost defies analysis. Tennyson, as one of those poets who have most remarkably restrained themselves to the *essential* domain of verse, not caring to write what prose might have had the power to execute, abounds with similar instances. In Shakespeare, too, who has by no means so restricted himself, but has torn up whole masses of the rough prose-world, and submitted them, as well as the finer matter of poetic phantasy, to the all-crushing power of his verse, we find examples of the same kind, hardly paralleled in the rest of literature. Thus, *ad aperturam,*—

> " Thou remember'st
> Since once I sat upon a promontory,
> And heard a mermaid on a dolphin's back,
> Uttering such dulcet and harmonious breath
> That the rude sea grew civil at her song,
> And certain stars shot madly from their spheres,
> To hear the sea-maid's music."

Again :—

> " Sit, Jessica ; look how the floor of heaven
> Is thick inlaid with patines **of** bright gold.
> There's not the smallest orb that thou behold'st.
> But in his motion like an angel sings,
> Still quiring to the young-eyed cherubims."

We will close this series of examples with a very apt
one from Milton, ·describing the loathsome appearance
of Sin and her brood at the gates of Hell.

> " Far less abhorred than these
> Vexed Scylla, bathing in the sea that parts
> Calabria from the hoarse Trinacrian shore ;
> Nor uglier follow the night-hag, when, called
> In secret, riding through the air she comes,
> Lured with the smell of infant blood, to dance
> With Lapland witches, while the labouring moon
> Eclipses at their charms."

All these examples seem to make it clear that there
belongs to verse a certain extreme arbitrariness of
imaginative association, sometimes taking the character
of mere light extravagance, sometimes leading to a
ghastly and unearthly effect, and often surprising the
mind with unexpected gleams of beauty and grandeur.
For, though we have already claimed for prose the
capability of pure grandeur and sublimity, we must
note here, in the interest of verse, that one source
of grandeur is this very license of most arbitrary
combination which verse gives.

Some light might, perhaps, be cast on this whole question of the relative and essential capabilities of verse and prose by a study of the law of Shakespeare's instinctive shiftings in his dramas between the two modes of writing. In such a study it would require to be premised that, as Shakespeare stands, by birth-right and choice, on the verse side of the river, and only makes occasional excursions to the prose side, it is to be expected that his practice will indicate rather the range within which prose has the sole title than the extent of ground over which it may expatiate as joint-proprietor. Forbearing for the present, how-ever, any such interesting inquiry, let us be content with the approximate conclusions to which we have independently come. These may be recapitulated as follows :— That in the whole vast field of the speculative and didactic, prose is the legitimate monarch, receiving verse but as a visitor and guest, who will carry back bits of rich ore and other specimens of the land's produce ; that in the great business of record, also, prose is pre-eminent, verse but voluntarily assisting; that in the expression of passion, and the work of moral stimulation, verse and prose meet as co-equals, prose undertaking the rougher and harder duty, where passion intermingles with the storm of current doctrine, and with the play and conflict of social interests—some-times, when thus engaged, bursting forth into such

strains of irregular music that verse takes up the echo
and prolongs it in measured modulation, leaving prose
rapt and listening to hear itself outdone; and, lastly,
that in the noble realm of poetry or imagination
prose also is capable of all exquisite, beautiful, powerful, and magnificent effects, but that, by reason of a
greater ease with fancies when they come in crowds,
and of a greater range and arbitrariness of combination,
verse here moves with the more royal gait. And thus
Prose and Verse are presented as two circles or spheres,
not entirely separate, as some would make them, but
intersecting and interpenetrating through a large portion of both their bulks, and disconnected only in
two crescents outstanding at the right and left, or,
if you adjust them differently, at the upper and lower
extremities. The left or lower crescent, the peculiar
and sole region of prose, is where we labour amid the
sheerly didactic or the didactic combined with the
practical and the stern; the right or upper crescent,
the peculiar and sole region of verse, is where $\pi\acute{a}\theta\eta\sigma\iota\varsigma$
at its utmost thrill and ecstasy interblends with the
highest and most daring $\pi o\acute{\iota}\eta\sigma\iota\varsigma$.

What Mr. De Quincey, in his clear and modest self-
appreciation, claims as one of his titles to a place in
English literature, if not as his most valued title, is
that, being expressly a prose writer, he has yet ad-

vanced farther into the peculiar and established domain
of verse, as we have just defined it, than almost any
other prose writer in the language. In the passage we
quoted from him at the beginning of the paper, he
represents himself as almost a unique artificer in
at least one department of impassioned and imaginative prose—that which partakes of the character of
personal confessions. In universal literature he can
refer but to one passage, in the *Confessions of St.
Augustine*, as coming within the same literary definition as parts of his own *Opium Eater* and of his *Suspiria
de Profundis*. This is likely to be true, because Mr.
De Quincey says it; but it is well to bear in mind (more
especially as there is a certain ambiguity in Mr. De
Quincey's expression—" the utter sterility of universal
literature in this one department of impassioned prose ")
—that, if there has not been much of impassioned prose-
writing of this one species, the literature of all languages contains noble specimens of impassioned and
imaginative prose of one kind or another. To name
the first example that occurs to us, Milton's prose
works contain passages of such grandeur as almost to
rival his poetry. Let the following stand as a specimen : it is the concluding passage of his pamphlet on
the *Causes that have hindered the Reformation in
England*, written in the form of an epistle to a friend.

" Oh! Sir, I do now feel myself enwrapt on the

sudden into those mazes and labyrinths of dreadful and
hideous thoughts that which way to get out or which
way to end I know not, unless I turn mine eyes, and,
with your help, lift up my hands, to that eternal and
propitious Throne where nothing is readier than grace
and refuge to the distresses of mortal suppliants; and
as it were a shame to leave these serious thoughts less
piously than the heathen were wont to conclude their
graver discourses—

"Thou, therefore, that sitst in light and glory un-
approachable, Parent of Angels and Men! next, thee I
implore, Omnipotent King, Redeemer of that lost remnant whose nature thou didst assume, Ineffable and
Everlasting Love! and Thou, the third subsistence
of Divine Infinitude, Illumining Spirit, the joy and
solace of created things!—one tri-personed Godhead!
look upon this thy poor and almost spent and expiring
Church; leave her not thus a prey to these importunate
wolves, that wait and think long till they devour thy
tender flock—these wild boars that have broke into thy
vineyard, and left the print of their polluting hoofs on
the souls of thy servants. Oh! let them not bring
about their damned designs that now stand at the
entrance of the bottomless pit, expecting the watchward
to open and let out those dreadful locusts and scorpions
to reinvolve us in that pitchy cloud of infernal darkness, where we shall never more see the sun of thy
truth again, never hope for the cheerful dawn, never
more hear the bird of morning sing. Be moved with
pity at the afflicted state of this our shaken monarchy,
that now lies labouring under her throes, and struggling
against the grudges of more dreaded calamities.

"Oh! Thou, that after the impetuous rage of five

bloody inundations and the succeeding sword of intes-
tine war, soaking the land in her own gore, didst pity
the sad and ceaseless revolution of our swift and thick-
coming sorrows—when we were quite breathless, didst
motion peace and terms of covenant with us, and,
having first well-nigh freed us from anti-Christian thral-
dom, didst build up this Britannic empire to a glorious
and enviable highth, with all her daughter islands about
her—stay us in this felicity; let not the obstinacy of
our half-obedience and will-worship bring forth that
viper of sedition that for these fourscore years hath
been breeding to eat through the entrails of our peace;
but let her cast her abortive spawn without the danger of
this travailing and throbbing kingdom, that we may still
remember, in our solemn thanksgivings, how for us the
northern ocean, even to the frozen Thule, was scattered
with the proud shipwrecks of the Spanish Armada, and
the very maw of hell ransacked, and made to give up
her concealed destruction, ere she could vent it in that
horrible and damned blast.

"Oh, how much more glorious will those former
deliverances appear, when we shall know them not only
to have saved us from greatest miseries past, but to
have reserved us for greatest happiness to come!
Hitherto Thou hast but freed us, and that not fully,
from the unjust and tyrannous chain of thy foes; now
unite us entirely, and appropriate us to Thyself; tie us
everlastingly in willing homage to the prerogative of
thy Eternal Throne.

"And now we know, O Thou, our most certain hope
and defence, that thine enemies have been consulting
all the sorceries of the Great Whore, and have joined
their plots with that sad intelligencing tyrant that

mischiefs the world with his mines of Ophir, and lies
thirsting to revenge his naval ruins that have larded
our seas : but let them all take counsel together, and
let it come to nought; let them decree and do Thou
cancel it; let them gather themselves and be scattered
let them embattle themselves and be broken; let them
embattle and be broken, for Thou art with us.

"Then, amidst the hymns and halleluiahs of saints,
some one may perhaps be heard offering at high strains,
in new and lofty measures, to sing and celebrate thy
divine mercies and marvellous judgments in this land
throughout all ages; whereby this great and warlike
nation, instructed and inured to the fervent and continual practice of truth and righteousness, and casting
far from her the rags of her old vices, may press on
hard to that high and happy emulation, to be found the
soberest, wisest, and most Christian people, at that day,
when Thou, the Eternal and shortly-expected King,
shalt open the clouds to judge the several kingdoms of
the world, and, distributing national honours and rewards to religious and just commonwealths, shalt put
an end to all earthly tyrannies, proclaiming the universal and mild monarchy through Heaven and Earth,
When they undoubtedly, that by their labours, counsels,
and prayers, have been earnest for the common good of
religion and their country, shall receive, above the inferior orders of the Blessed, the regal addition of Prin-
cipalities, Legions, and Thrones, into their glorious
titles, and, in supereminence of beatific vision progres-
sing the dateless and irrevoluble circle of eternity, shall
clasp inseparable hands with joy and bliss in over measure for ever. But they, contrary, that by the impairing
and diminution of the true faith, the distresses and

servitude of their country, aspire to high dignity, rule, and promotion here, after a shameful end in this life (which God grant them!) shall be thrown down eternally into the darkest and deepest gulf of Hell, where, under the despiteful control, the trample and spurn of all the other Damned, that in the anguish of their tortures shall have no other ease than to exercise a raving and bestial tyranny over them as their slaves and negroes, they shall remain in that plight for ever, the basest, the lowermost, the most dejected, most underfoot and down-trodden vassals of Perdition."

This may pass as a specimen of *impassioned* prose hardly to be matched in the English language. For specimens of what may more properly be called *imaginative* prose we might refer also to English writers, and to some English writers now living. But in this connexion it is perhaps fairest to name that foreign writer who, by the general consent of literary Europe, is accounted *facile princeps* among all prose invaders of the peculiar dominion of verse—the German Jean Paul. All who are acquainted with the writings of Jean Paul must be aware that, whatever is to be said of his genius as a whole or in comparison with that of his compatriot Goethe, in the single faculty of wild and rich prose-poesy he is the most astonishing even of German writers. Passages verifying this might be quoted in scores from his fictions. The famous dream of *Christ and the Universe* is perhaps his grandest and most daring phantasy of the kind;

and, had we space, we should quote it. We will quote instead, a shorter and less awful passage—the singularly beautiful conclusion of the novel of *Quintus Fixlein,* describing the solitary walk homewards of a man who has just left two dear friends.

" We were all of us too deeply moved. We at last tore ourselves asunder from repeated embraces; my friend retired with the soul whom he loves. I remained alone behind him with the Night.

" And I walked without aim through woods, through valleys, and over brooks, and through sleeping villages, to enjoy the great Night like a Day. I walked, and still looked, like the magnet, to the region of midnight, to strengthen my heart at the gleaming twilight, at this upstretching aurora of a morning beneath our feet. While night butterflies flitted, white blossoms fluttered, white stars fell, and the white snow-powder hung silvery in the high shadow of the Earth, which reaches beyond the Moon, and which is our Night. Then began the Æolian harp of creation to tremble and to sound, blown on from above; and my immortal soul was a string in this harp. The heart of a brother, everlasting Man, swelled under the everlasting Heaven, as the seas swell under the sun and under the moon. The distant village clock struck midnight, mingling, as it were, with the ever-pealing tone of ancient Eternity. The limbs of my buried ones touched cold on my soul, and drove away its blots, as dead hands heal eruptions of the skin. I walked silently through little hamlets, and close by their outer churchyards, where crumbled upcast coffin-boards were glimmering, while the once-bright eyes that had lain in them were mouldered into

grey ashes. Cold thought! clutch not like a cold
spectre at my heart : I look up to the starry sky, and
an everlasting chain stretches thither, and over, and
below ; and all is life, and warmth, and light, and all
is Godlike or God.

"Towards morning I descried thy late lights, little
city of my dwelling, which I belong to on this side the
grave ; I returned to the earth ; and in the steeples,
behind the by-advanced great midnight, it struck half-
past two. About this hour, in 1794, Mars went down
in the west, and the moon rose in the east; and my
soul desired, in grief for the noble warlike blood which
is still streaming on the blossoms of spring : ' Ah,
retire, bloody War, like red Mars ; and thou, still Peace,
come forth, like the mild divided moon.' "—MR. CAR-
LYLE'S *Translation.*

Even after such a passage as this there are passages
in Mr. De Quincey's writings the power of which, as
specimens of skill in impassioned and imaginative
prose, would be felt as something new. His *Confessions,*
his *Suspiria de Profundis,* and even his present volumes
of *Autobiographic Sketches,* contain passages which, for
weird beauty, and for skill in embodying the impal-
pable and the visionary, are not surpassed anywhere in
poetry. Take the following as an example : it is an
attempt to impersonate and generalize in distinct living
shapes those various forms or powers of sorrow that hold
dominion over man and human life. As there are
three Graces, three Fates, and three Furies, so, says
De Quincey, there are three Ladies of Sorrow :—

"THE THREE LADIES OF SORROW.

"The eldest of the three is named *Mater Lachry-marum*, Our Lady of Tears. She it is that night and day raves and moans, calling for vanished faces. She stood in Rama, when a voice was heard of lamentation —'Rachel weeping for her children and refusing to be comforted.' She it was that stood in Bethlehem on the night when Herod's sword swept its nurseries of innocents, and the little feet were stiffened for ever, which, heard at times as they tottered along floors overhead, woke pulses of love in household hearts that were not unmarked in heaven. Her eyes are sweet and subtle, wild and sleepy by turns; oftentimes rising to the clouds; oftentimes challenging the heavens. She wears a diadem round her head. And I knew by childish memories that she could go abroad upon the winds, when she heard the sobbing of litanies or the thundering of organs, and when she beheld the mustering of summer clouds. This sister, the elder, it is that carries keys more than Papal at her girdle, which open every cottage and every palace. She, to my knowledge, sate all last summer by the bedside of the blind beggar, him that so often and so gladly I talked with, whose pious daughter, eight years old, with the sunny countenance, resisted the temptations of play and village mirth to travel all day long on dusty roads with her afflicted father. For this did God send her a great reward. In the spring-time of the year, and whilst yet her own spring was budding, He took her to Himself. But her blind father mourns for ever over *her;* still he dreams at midnight that the little guiding hand is locked within his own; and still he wakens to a darkness that is *now* within a second and a deeper darkness. This *Mater*

Lachrymarum also has been sitting all this winter of 1844-45 within the bedchamber of the Czar, bringing before his eyes a daughter (not less pious) that vanished to God not less suddenly, and left behind her a darkness not less profound. By the power of her keys is it that Our Lady of Tears glides, a ghostly intruder, into the chambers of sleepless men, sleepless women, sleepless children, from Ganges to the Nile, from Nile to Mississippi; and her, because she is the first-born of her house, and has the widest empire, let us honour with the title of 'Madonna.'

"The second sister is called *Mater Suspiriorum*, Our Lady of Sighs. She neither scales the clouds, nor walks abroad upon the winds. She wears no diadem. And her eyes, if they were ever seen, would be neither sweet nor subtle; no man could read their story; they would be found filled with perishing dreams and with wrecks of forgotten delirium. But she raises not her eyes; her head, on which sits a dilapidated turban, droops for ever—for ever fastens on the dust. She weeps not. She groans not. But she sighs inaudibly at intervals. Her sister, Madonna, is oftentimes stormy and frantic—raging in the highest against heaven, and demanding back her darlings. But Our Lady of Sighs never clamours, never defies, dreams not of rebellious aspirations. She is humble to abjectness. Hers is the meekness that belongs to the hopeless. Murmur she may, but it is in her sleep. Whisper she may, but it is to herself in the twilight. Mutter she does at times, but it is in solitary places that are desolate as she is desolate, in ruined cities, and when the sun has gone down to rest. This sister is the visitor of the Pariah, of the Jew, of the bondsman to the oar in Mediterranean galleys, of the English criminal in Norfolk Island, blotted out from remembrance in sweet far-off England, of the baffled penitent reverting his eye for ever upon a solitary grave, which to him seems the altar over-thrown of some past and bloody sacrifice, on which altar no oblations can now be availing, whether towards pardon that he might implore, or towards reparation that he might attempt. Every slave that at noonday looks up to the tropical sun with timid reproach, as he points with one hand to the earth our general mother, but for *him* a stepmother, as he points with the other hand to the Bible, our general teacher, but against *him* sealed and sequestered;—every woman sitting in darkness, without love to shelter her head, or hope to illume her solitude, because the heaven-born instincts kindling in her nature germs of holy affections, which God implanted in her womanly bosom, having been stifled by social necessities, now burn sullenly to waste, like sepulchral lamps among the ancients;—every nun defrauded of her unreturning May-time by wicked kinsmen, whom God will judge:—every captive in every dungeon;—all that are betrayed, and all that are rejected, outcasts by traditionary law, and children of *hereditary* disgrace—all these walk with ' Our Lady of Sighs.' She also carries a key; but she needs it little. For her kingdom is chiefly among the tents of shame, and the houseless vagrant of every clime. Yet in the very highest ranks of men she finds chapels of her own ; and even in glorious England there are some that, to the world, carry their heads as proudly as the reindeer, who yet secretly have received her mark upon their foreheads.

" But the third sister, who is also the youngest— !

Hush! whisper, whilst we talk of *her!* Her kingdom
is not large, or else no flesh should live; but within
that kingdom all power is hers. Her head, turreted
like that of Cybele, rises almost beyond the reach of
night. She droops not; and her eyes, rising so high,
might be hidden by distance. But, being what they
are, they cannot be hidden; through the treble veil of
crape which she wears, the fierce light of a blazing
misery, that rests not for matins or for vespers—for
noon of day, or noon of night—for ebbing or for flowing tide—may be read from the very ground. She is
the defier of God. She is also the mother of lunacies
and the suggestress of suicides. Deep lie the roots of
her power; but narrow is the nation that she rules. For
she can approach only those in whom a profound nature
has been upheaved by central convulsions; in whom the
heart trembles and the brain rocks under conspiracies of
tempest from without and tempest from within. Madonna moves with uncertain steps, fast or slow, but still
with tragic grace. Our Lady of Sighs creeps timidly
and stealthily. But this youngest sister moves with
incalculable motions, bounding, and with tiger's leaps.
She carries no key; for, though coming rarely amongst
men, she storms all doors at which she is permitted to
enter at all. And *her* name is *Mater Tenebrarum*, Our
Lady of Darkness."

In this noble piece of prose, as in the passages from
Milton and Richter, no one can fail to remark, in exact
accordance with what has been advanced in the course
of this essay, that, precisely as the passion gains in
force and intensity, and the pure process of poetic

combination transacts itself with ease and vigour, the
language acquires and sustains a more decided metrical
cadence. It would not be difficult to arrange parts of
the passages so that what has been printed as prose
should present to the eye the appearance of irregular
verse. And so, generally, a peculiar rhythm or music
will always be found in highly impassioned or imaginative prose. The voice swells with its burthen ; the
hand rises and falls ; the foot beats time. And thus,
as we have more than once said, prose passes into verse
by visible gradations. Still, there is a clear line of
separation between the most metrical prose and what
is conventionally recognised as verse ; and with all the
great effects that may be produced on this side of the
line of separation, Prose, as such, is entitled to be
credited. And why should not prose do its utmost ?
Why should we not have more men like Richter and
De Quincey, to teach prose its uses and capabilities ?
"The muse of prose-literature," we have ventured to
say on another occasion, "has been very hardly dealt
with. We see not why, in prose, there should not be
much of that license in the fantastic, that measured
riot, that right of whimsy, that unabashed dalliance
with the extreme and the beautiful, which the world
allows, by prescription, to verse. Why may not prose
chase forest-nymphs, and see little green-eyed elves,
and delight in peonies and musk-roses, and invoke the

stars, and roll mists about the hills, and watch the seas
thundering through caverns and dashing against the
promontories ?   Why, in prose, quail from the grand
or ghastly on the one hand, or blush with shame at too
much of the exquisite on the other ? Is Prose made
of iron ?   Must it never weep, never laugh, never
linger to look at a buttercup, never ride at a gallop over
the downs ?   Always at a steady trot, transacting only
such business as may be done within the limits of a
soft sigh on the one hand and a thin smile on the other,
must it leave all finer and higher work of imagination to the care of Verse ? "   All speed, then, to the
prose invasion of the peculiar realm of verse !   The
farther the conquest can proceed, perhaps the better in
the end for both parties.   The time is perhaps coming
when the best prose shall be more like verse than it
now is, and the best verse shall not disdain a certain
resemblance to prose.

A word in conclusion, to prevent misconception. We
have tried to define the special and peculiar domain of
Verse ; but we have scrupulously avoided saying anything that would imply an opinion that Verse may not,
both lawfully and with good effect, go beyond that
domain. We have all along supposed the contrary.
Verse, merely as a form of expression, has charms of
its own. A thought, an incident, or a feeling, which

may be perfectly well expressed in prose, may be rendered more pleasing, more impressive, and more memorable, by being expressed in metre or rhyme. If a man has some doctrine or theory which he wishes to expound, there is no reason, if he finds it possible, and chooses to take the trouble, why he should not make the exposition a metrical one; and, if his verses are good, there is every probability that, on account of the public relish for metre in itself, his exposition will take a more secure place in literature than would have been attained by a corresponding piece of didactic prose. So also a witticism, or a description, or a plain, homely story, may often be delivered more neatly, tersely, and delightfully, if it comes in the garb of verse. In the same way, a man may often impress more powerfully some strongly-felt sentiment by throwing it into a series of nervous and hearty lines. In short, we ought to be ready to accept wit in metre, or narrative in metre, or politics in metre, or anything else in metre, when we can get it; and we ought, in every such case, to allow all the additional credit to the author which is due to his skill in so delightful an art as versification. Much of the poetry of Horace, all the satires of Juvenal, the *Hudibras* of Butler, Pope's metrical essays, and many other compositions of tolerably diverse kinds, may be cited as examples of that order of poetry which consists of shrewdness, wit, manly feeling, and general intellectual vigour, manifesting themselves in metre. Who does not admire the literary felicity displayed in such works, and who, having them in his mind, can remain insensible to the claims of verse to range at large wherever it chooses to go? What we wish to make clear, however, is that a distinction may and must be drawn between verse considered as an essential condition of a peculiar kind of thought and verse considered as an optional form of expression which may be chosen, in almost any case, for the sake of its fine and elegant effects. The fact that verse may be regarded in this latter aspect is perhaps the sole justification of nine-tenths of what is called poetry in all languages.

THE END.